Budget Ninjas

Providing Instant Relief
For Financial Pressure

Dennis K. Byrd

i

SECOND EDITION

ISBN: 1523826401
ISBN-13: 978-1523826407

BUDGET NINJAS

DEDICATION

To all those that are tired of living paycheck to paycheck, this book is for you.

Contents

INTRODUCTION

Are you tired of always being broke? Is your paycheck already spent before you can cash it? *Budget Ninjas* will help you gain control of your personal finances and help you understand where all your money is going. *Budget Ninjas* will equip you with the tools and knowledge you need to successfully manage your money.

I know from personal experience that no one likes to be told, "Sorry, you can't buy that because we are on a budget." That's not what this book is about. This book is about helping you discover how you can pay the bills you owe on time, purchase the things you need when you need them, minimize the impact of unexpected bills, and plan for and achieve the dreams of your future.

You might have tried to budget before, but it never worked out. Sometimes the financial pressure is just too great. Maybe you thought you didn't make enough money to be on a budget or didn't think one was necessary. You might have tried some accounting software or some other computer program to help, but that didn't work either because of the massive amount of time required to understand how it worked. It's easy to understand why so many people choose to live without a budget and struggle to make ends meet.

After reading *Budget Ninjas*, you'll be able to answer tough questions like these: "Am I going to have enough money to pay my bills this month?" or "Will I be able to put my child through college?" or "Can I really afford this new house or car?" After all, that's what budgeting is all about, isn't it? This book is about giving you the knowledge you need to make intelligent decisions about your money, to make it through the most difficult times, and to plan for and achieve goals you might have thought impossible.

In the end, you will have confidence. You will have peace. You will be amazed at what you have accomplished. Are you ready to get started? Are you ready for some instant relief?

Whether you are reading this by yourself or participating in a small group study, the following 10-week lessons are guaranteed to open your eyes to a whole new world of opportunities.

WEEK 1 - WELCOME TO BUDGETING

In the following weeks, you will slowly transform from a budget zero to a budget hero. Carefully read through the material presented. Be diligent to complete the required work. Participate in group discussions if you are doing this as part of a group study. Each exercise is designed to bring you step by step to the ultimate goal of financial freedom.

Those who complete this course will earn the title of a Budget Ninja. What in the world is a budget ninja anyway? A budget is easy to describe. Most people believe and understand that a budget is a tool that is used to help them manage their money. Is it fair to say that if someone is good at controlling their spending, and is able to save a little money for the future, that person is good at money management? That's great, but seems to be lacking in the excitement department. A person that lives on a budget may appear to others as boring, controlled, and weak.

A ninja is easy to describe as well. You've seen them in movies before, dressed in black, using stealth and acrobatic maneuvers to get to their destination. They are in and out before you know it. No one can stand in their way. We perceive them as masters of weaponry, confident, invincible, and driven. They get the job done. They live a life of mystery and intrigue.

What I want for you is to combine the characteristics of a ninja with the power of a budget to create an army of individuals that leave the world around them with their jaws gaping wide, wondering in amazement how they are able to do the things they do. You hear the sound of them, but you do not know where they come from or where they are going. All you see is the impact they left behind. Others will begin to notice the change in you and want to join in on the excitement and experience the power of a budget ninja.

In martial arts, a student must master many disciplines before they can advance to higher degrees. Typically, many months or years of study and practice are required to become competent and to rise to the level of "master". Students spend their time training in a dojo, where they can concentrate and work on perfecting their skills. You'll complete your training in the following 10 weeks as you complete each chapter. We will quickly teach you advanced budgeting concepts. You will practice and sharpen your budgeting skills and build a real budget at our web site, **www.budgetsteward.com**, using our free **Budget Master Online Service**.

Before jumping online to create your first budget, you need to understand the concepts taught in this book so that you have the foundational knowledge you need in order to make it really work like you want it and need it to. Even though you are given all the tools you need, if you don't know exactly what you are building or why you are building it, you are likely to waste time and material building something that's not going to be very useful, or at least as useful as it could have been. There are a number of ways to build a budget, and you need to understand what options are available to you. You need to master the weapons we give you. With time, you'll understand the power that you can use to accomplish almost anything.

A DIFFERENT KIND OF BUDGET

There are hundreds of budget programs out there. A budget can be as simple as an envelope that is used to hold money for a particular purpose, such as groceries. You might find a budget program on your smart phone to help you keep track of what you spend as you spend it. A budget program could be nothing more than a simple spreadsheet on a computer or on a piece of paper on which you write down your list of bills. You can find many accounting software packages that help with budgeting and get down to the fine details of every transaction you make. Do any of these budgets give you the answers you are looking for? Are they helping you make life decisions and prepare for the future? How do you know if a particular budget program is right for you? You will know a budgeting system is right for you when it serves the purpose it was built for, and that purpose is defined by you.

That's what makes the *Budget Ninjas* process different. *Budget Ninjas* considers the "human" element. Together, we think about the reasons why you want and need a budget. Your budget is built for that purpose. Some of you are going through some very rough and troubling times. For you, the purpose of a budget is to first figure out how to pay for all the bills you have. You may have had a lender take your last dime without thinking twice about the impact that action had on your family. You might have begged for more time so you could come up with money before they repossessed your property. You cried as they gave you that cold, hard look and said, "Sorry, it's not personal." Sure, it wasn't personal to them, but it sure was personal to you as you thought about where your next meal was going to come from or how you were going put some gas in your car. That's enough to make anyone an emotional wreck.

The last thing you need right now is a ten-step program that treats everyone the same regardless of their circumstances, running them through the same mind-numbing exercises that seem pointless and take forever to see any results. You don't need a "do this and do that and all will be well" book. You need someone who can walk with you as you take on this new adventure and journey of real budgeting. I hope to be that person by sharing a little bit of my life with you, relating the struggles I had to go through, and giving you some ideas of things that worked for me and others I have coached. I hope my stories will make you think and perhaps even bring a smile to your face. I hope you will see your budget come alive as it has for me, opening your eyes to a whole new world of possibilities. I've sat down with many families in one-on-one financial coaching sessions over the years, plowing through the details of how those families managed their money. In nearly all cases, everyone had the same goal, and that goal was trying to find more money. Your typical family is just trying to make ends meet like everyone else, doing their best to become smarter in the ways of handling money. Most cannot see the world of opportunities that lies beyond the mountain of debt they have in front of them. They start to climb out of debt only to be pushed back down the hill by a landslide of unexpected bills. *Budget Ninjas* will teach you how to secure lifelines to your finances so when the unexpected happens, you don't lose ground as you climb over that mountain of debt.

The ultimate purpose of *Budget Ninjas* is <u>not</u> to get you focused on your finances, but to get you into a position where you don't have to be. I'm sure you have seen and heard plenty of folks who like to give you every detail of what possessions they have and how much they spent on this or that, seeming almost obsessed over their financial standing and the material things of this world. It can hurt to hear their stories and latest conquests because you start to wonder where you went wrong in life, what mistakes you have made that brought you to this point, and trying to justify why you are not in as good financial shape as they are. I'd rather not turn you into a person like that. I'd rather get you to the point where you don't have to worry about money or bills and are able to focus on the things that make you really happy and on achieving the dreams that you have. Don't get me wrong. I've got the budgeting process down to a fine science. The *Budget Ninjas* way <u>will</u> work, but let's first set the stage and think about a few things before we start.

Don't be fooled by what others are telling you. Many material possessions are easily hidden behind a mountain of debt. Many will claim they love their jobs, but some are forced to spend 50 to 60 hours a week working overtime or two or more jobs, while all along they are really worn out, miserably stressed, and trying to earn just enough money to make minimum payments on all their credit cards. Relatives especially will go the extra mile to try and fool you into thinking how well off they are. Don't be afraid to tell the truth about where you stand financially. There's nothing wrong with being open and honest. When your best friend asks you to play a round of golf or go on a shopping trip, don't be afraid to tell him or her that you just had to replace the battery in your car and don't need to spend any extra money right now.

You may have friends and relatives that are in worse financial shape than you. Many of them won't tell you the truth when they come to you asking to borrow money, because if the truth be known, it would be very easy to see where they had simply overspent their money on frivolous things for themselves. Some families have repeat offenders in their lives, always asking for a handout. You avoid them because you know they are going to be asking you for a little more money just so they can "get by". I don't have a problem helping a person that is truly in need through no fault of their own and sometimes even if it is their fault, as long as they have learned their lesson. One easy way to really help that person is to first ask them if they are on a budget and, if they say no, to help them build one so both of you can understand why they are always in such bad shape. Of course, you'll need to learn how to build your own budget first! If they really want your hard-earned money, you have every right to ask for details. In fact, I might go as far to say you might be negligent in your duties as a friend or family member if you just give them a handout without conditions. You are what some might call an enabler, giving them a temporary financial fix even though you know that they will be back again for more at a later time. I'm sure most of you have heard that old saying, "Give a man a fish and he eats for a day; teach a man to fish and he eats for life." Instead of taking the easy way out for both of you, spend a little time to work on the problem. If they are open and honest with you and accept your offer to help them build a budget (or if they show you the budget they have), you'll both be much happier in the end. If you are the "bad apple" or one of those that frequently asks your family and friends for a contribution to your cause, I applaud you for reading this book, because that fact tells me you really want to learn to fish for yourself, stand on your own two feet, and make a better life for yourself.

The bad financial practices I have just described may be a lifestyle habit for some of you. Nothing is harder to break than a habit developed over many years. Habits come in many forms other than the usual suspects of smoking and drinking. The way we think and react is often habitual. We do the same things over and over, not even realizing we are creatures of habit. Think about when you get up in the morning. Do you ever think about changing the order of how you get ready for work? Have you ever thought about brushing your teeth before you get in the shower? Why do you always put the right sock on before the left sock? It really is funny the way our minds work. I'm going to ask you to be open-minded about some of the ideas I share. Try to think outside of the box.

Each week, we will focus on a particular area of your budget. You will learn specific skills and prepare material so that when you reach the final weeks, you can put it all together and build your first working budget. Don't be tempted to skip to the end and start working on your budget without first having the foundational knowledge you need to make it work right.

I have prepared a little test to see how open you are to thinking in different ways. It's a fun simple test that really drives many people nuts as they try to think outside of the box. Look at the picture in Figure 1-1. Can you connect the nine dots with only four straight lines without lifting your pencil once you start drawing? Give it a shot! It can be done, but you'll have to think outside of the box. If you can't figure it out, look at the end of the book for the answer.

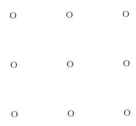

FIGURE 1-1

A HARD LIFE

You can see it in their faces. They are completely stressed out over the lack of money. Living paycheck to paycheck is not exactly the American dream that many had hoped for. Could you be one of those individuals? You never seem to get anywhere. It's been years since you took a nice vacation, or perhaps you have never taken one. Instead of living in the land of the free, you feel trapped and enslaved, suffocating beneath the mound of debt that never seems to go away. The pain is real. It seems like everyone else is living high on the hog. Where are these people getting so much money to blow? Why does it seem like you are the only one that is struggling, while everyone else is buying name-brand shoes and clothes? You start to question everything. "Do I need a new job making more money?" "Do I need to go back to school and learn a new trade?" If you aren't thinking that, your spouse is and reminding you all the time, adding to the stress you already have. All you want to do is provide for your family, giving them the things they need and hoping to offer them a better life than the one you had. However, there's always something coming up or breaking down. If it's not the school wanting more money for a project or field trip, then it's an unexpected spike in the power bill, a dentist visit, or a vet bill that leaves you with little money to do anything. Things break. One day, I pulled out the vacuum cleaner to clean out my mini-van. Shortly after I turned it on, the vacuum sucked up something hard (probably a penny) and before I knew it, I heard the crunching of plastic as the part that spins and causes the vacuum to work crumbled. It's hard not to throw up your hands in defeat. It's almost too much to bear sometimes, looking at the constant parade of people ready to pick money out of your pocket.

Young folks struggle to find meaningful employment, even with a college degree. Many are questioning whether a college education is really worth all the money you have to pay in order to get your degree. Many can only find part-time work because companies today do not want to pay for all the benefits for a full-time employee, like health insurance, taxes, unemployment insurance, etc. Many young couples are already carrying a heavy burden of student loans, car loans, and other debt that comes from just getting married. In fact, paying for the wedding itself can be a tremendous burden once you count the cost of securing the place, the reception, photography, wedding rings, invitations, flowers, entertainment, attire, and of course, the honeymoon! You can easily spend tens of thousands of dollars on a wedding that lasts no longer than half an hour. Unless you are one of the lucky ones, you'll have to foot a big portion of this bill yourself. I really believe that a newlywed couple who can enter marriage debt free is much more likely to have a happy marriage and will have a greater chance of growing old together. Unfortunately, the majority of couples won't make it too long before ending up in divorce court, which will land them further in debt. They don't know how to handle the stress of financial pressure and end up taking it out on each other. Arguing over money (or the lack thereof) is the number one reason for divorces today. The deck is stacked against young couples and no one seems to know what to do. The most important rules for those wanting to get married, however, are be open and honest with each other, know how to do a budget, and communicate!

Middle aged couples have it especially hard. Although you are battle hardened and you've made it through the tough, early years of marriage, a fresh wave of financial mortar bombs is about to hit. You're making a little more money, but you have more and more bills that take every dime you have. Your kids are growing up and must have everything their friends have. The cost of all those technological gadgets has skyrocketed. Once you or your kids obtain one of those gadgets, it will soon be outdated and need to be replaced with a newer, better, and faster one. It's amazing how smart these companies are, saving a few enhancements for the next release to entice you to buy or upgrade to the new one only a few months after you just bought the old device. College for kids is quickly approaching and you haven't saved the first dollar. Some folks may make a decent amount of money, but they have a decent number of bills as well, and hardly any money is left to pay for college. Your kids want cars to help relieve you of the carpool madness. It sounds like a great idea until you realize there's no money to pay for the car, the insurance, the taxes, and the traffic tickets!

When my daughter obtained her license, we helped her get her first car, a nice used car that our mechanic gave a passing grade. To her credit, she said she did not want a new car because she was afraid of getting a scratch on it (and because we told her we would not be purchasing a new car for her). Insurance wasn't bad while I was still listed as the primary driver of the car. That all changed, though, when she got her license. The insurance more than doubled, and that was after her safe driving discount, good grade discount, driver training discount, multi-line discount, multi-vehicle discount, and gender discount! For my son, it was worse! Apparently, boys lose a few IQ points when they get behind the wheel of a vehicle and insurance companies have to charge more. Needless to say, a little planning is needed here, especially if your own car has half a million miles on it, you owe more than it's worth, and it barely gets you where you want to go.

If you are not spending money on the kids, you are spending money on your parents. Your parents are getting older, requiring more of your attention, your time, and perhaps even your money. If there is any money left for you and your spouse, it's a miracle. Since the money is gone, your life ebbs into a deep rut. To make matters worse, your spouse has now officially entered into a mid-life crisis, spending money like it's nobody's business in order to impress the younger crowd. Where's your excitement? Where's the money to even have a little bit of fun? The honeymoon is over. The drudgery of day-to-day living can really start to get on one's nerves. The only excitement you have to look forward to is the next brawl over bills!

It is also at this stage of life when many are faced with a challenge. Do we take what money is left over and spend it now, enjoying what life has to offer, or do we store it all away for a rainy day or for retirement? These days it seems there will be no social security left when we are older. Even though we have paid into it year after year, the government continues to squander it on other programs, risking the livelihood of future generations. So, do you put away as much as you can in a 401K or I.R.A.? If you do, do you know how to balance your investments so they can survive the volatility of the stock market? What happens when the stock market crashes? One year, my boss was ready to retire, but the stock market was hit hard. He ended up having to work several more years because all the money he had saved so diligently quickly vanished.

There is so much to think about, so much to consider, so much to keep track of. That's why you need the help of a budget to help you see what you can and can't do. The younger crowd is definitely focused on enjoying life now, as I believe they should be. They are young, energetic, and can do almost anything they set their minds to. The elderly are also focused on trying to enjoy the remaining days of their lives. Unfortunately, there are many things their bodies no longer permit them to do. What good is it for them to have saved money all this time only to find out that they can't do the things they wanted to do when they were younger? That's the struggle middle age folks have. There is so much left to be done, yet so much to take care of now. It really is hard.

Older folks don't have it any easier. You saved hard for retirement and invested heavily in your 401K, only to find those saving evaporate like a rain drop on a hot grill when the stock market takes a plunge. Through no fault of your own, your entire savings could be wiped out by a few hospital visits, just as my mother's savings disappeared after an automobile accident. Insurance only covers so much. Your monthly check is all you have for now, until the government hits you up with a new fee that chips away at what little is left. It never seems to last the whole month and you find yourself going hungry on the last days. Your grown-up kids are struggling financially too, so you don't want to bother them for help. What is there to look forward to?

Even the so-called wealthy have it rough. Many live in million-dollar houses yet don't have enough spare change to buy a hot dog. I heard one lady describe how she was ready to sell her house and start all over because she couldn't make ends meet, even with a salary over $350,000 a year. What's wrong with this picture?

I'm not even going to talk about single parents. You're in a category all by yourself, no pun intended. You don't need a budget survival guide; with everything you have to deal with, you need a life survival guide. However, I think this book is a good place to start, so keep reading.

A DIFFERENT PERSPECTIVE

I hated to paint such a picture of gloom and doom, but the fact is, what I have just described is "life as we know it" for a good many folks. No matter where you are in life, there's always pressure either to maintain your financial and social status or to do better. That's not necessarily a bad goal, but what does it mean to "do better"? I have yet to meet a person who is completely content with where he is in his life. Why is that? Many times, growing up, I was told to be happy with what I had. Why are so many people suffering terribly from the pain of financial pressures, unhappy with where they are in life? Is it because they do not have enough money to put food on the table? Are they wearing raggedy clothes and shoes? I have been lucky enough in my working life to make a little more money every year but one. I have also discovered that every year, I have expenses that increase at the exact same pace that my income did. Have I done better by increasing my capacity to obtain "things"? Have these things made me a better person or made me happier? I have noticed that my most expensive possessions require the most expensive repairs, bringing with them an additional level of anxiety hoping they don't break down. You know something is wrong when the cost to replace the battery in your luxury car is more than your mortgage payment.

Some of the most stressful times of my life were trying to figure out how I was going to pay for possessions I had acquired with loans, possessions that were now breaking down, like my own car. You may also experience stress when you purchase a new car. You know that the moment you drive it off the parking lot, it is going to be worth less than the amount you just paid for it. After the recent housing bubble, many found themselves in a similar situation with their houses. Their mortgage balances were more than the price their houses could sell for—a circumstance called an upside-down mortgage. Where does it all end? When can we stop the pursuit of things? There is an answer, but it is not obvious to everyone.

I now realize that when I was a child, we were poor and didn't have much money. My dad made about $7 an hour, which was not a lot of money to live on if you think about it. My mom stayed home with us four boys. I was the youngest. I had a fun childhood, though. Those were some of the best times of my life, playing with little cars in the gravel by the road, playing in the woods, and building play forts. Before I started school back in the early 1970s, my parents moved into a house in the small town of Williamsburg, Indiana. It was a decent size home, over one hundred years old, and it didn't have indoor plumbing. If you wanted some water, you took a bucket out to the pump and pumped it out by hand. If you wanted to use the restroom, you went to the outhouse.

We were poor, but nobody told me, so I was ok with it and I was happy. It's really strange, but my mom and dad seemed happy too. I don't remember any fights over the lack of money or the lack of things. I thought we were actually kind of well off. My dad would come home from work and we would all be waiting for him in the living room, watching one of the three channels we received on our little black-and-white TV. Every now and then, he would dig into his pockets for whatever loose change he had and throw it wildly into the air sending all us four boys into a mad scramble trying to get our fair share. There was no fighting over what you ended up with; it was all fair game. I'd usually get a nickel or quarter and go straight across the street and buy some candy from the only store we had in town. Eating out at a restaurant was a luxury. We went to get fast food about once a month. Even so, I never went hungry. So, it stands to reason that having more money and things doesn't necessarily make one happier, right?

Necessity really is the mother of invention. My grandpa was always telling me he was going to build a big boat and buy an airplane someday and take us for rides around the world. Of course, that never happened, but I always dreamed of the day when it would. There was always something to look forward to. We worked with what we had and enjoyed every minute of it. I wonder whether we are taking away the dreams of our kids by giving them everything they could ask or think. What's left for them to dream about? How is their creativity being put to the test? What do they have to look forward to? It seems as though many teens have already experienced the world before they even graduate from high school. Without vision or dreams, where is the motivation to do better? How are they being challenged to be resourceful and work with what they already have? Being resourceful is a skill everyone needs as an adult to make the most of what you have. When your children are all grown up, they won't have you to give them everything they ask for just because they asked for it. When they are under the gun at work being asked to get something done that doesn't look possible, they'll have to tap the resourcefulness they developed as children. Don't deprive your kids of opportunities to develop this skill.

I truly believe the skills I learned as a kid were a direct result of not having everything handed to me on a silver platter. We were always experimenting, creating homemade games and toys from the little things we had on hand. My cousin lived about half a block away from where I lived. We each had a bedroom on the second floor. One day, we took a kite string and stretched it over the road, through a neighbor's yard and up to our windows and attached cups to the ends. What fun it was to talk on our newly created phones! Another time, we created a mini-carnival out of scraps of material we found in the garage. We would charge a nickel to play the game, and if you won, you might get an old match-box car as a prize. Ask your kids, if you have any, what fun they have created for themselves lately. Let them play in the dirt and woods. No telling what immunities to germs I built up over the years playing in such conditions!

Living in hard times is a relative concept. Ask someone in a war-ravaged part of the world, where good drinking water and food is scarce and there is a constant threat of violence. I'm sure they would love to trade places with many of us that think we are living in hard times. Many Americans would say they are living in hard times, yet if you try to get them to cancel the cable channels or take away their cell phone, you'll have a fight on your hands. Are they really living in rough times, or are they choosing to live paycheck to paycheck in order to keep the life of luxury they are currently enjoying? Try to keep it all in perspective when working your budget and ask yourself whether what you are trying to accomplish is the right thing to do.

CHANGING TIMES

Can anyone remember the good old days when paying for something in cash was normal? Nowadays, people will look at you strangely as you try to exchange cold hard cash for goods and services. "Swipe" used to be a term used by crooks who stole something from you. In today's computerized and mechanized world, "swipe" is now the magical term for taking your credit card or bank card and sliding it through a magnetic reader so you can charge your purchase. Soon, there will probably be a time when cash will be a thing of the past and we will all use electronic debits and credits. How times have changed.

In the past, when you got paid, you received a real check, you went to a real bank to cash the check, and you received real money. You would take your money and dole it out buying this and that. When the money was gone, it was gone. You simply waited until next week for your next paycheck and made do with what you had for the rest of the week. Of course, back then, what most families had in the way of material possessions wasn't much compared to today's lifestyle. No cell phones. No cable or satellite television with high definition channels to worry about. No gyms to attend. Credit cards were rare. How I miss the joys of a simplified lifestyle. If you are ever lucky enough to make it to Washington, DC, be sure to visit the American History Museum at the National Mall and look at how folks lived in times past. Look at the simplicity of their lives. It reminds me of my old family pictures in which we are all sitting around the table, playing board games. I wondered to myself whether any of us today could survive in a time like that now that we have been exposed to today's wonders of modern technology. What was life like before the invention of blogs or social networks?

Today, many don't even carry cash, and it's not because they don't have access to any. They rely solely on their bank cards or credit cards, or online banking, or some combination of it all. The same principle is still true though. You get paid. You dole it out (using your card or online purchases) buying this and that. Unfortunately, there is nothing to tell you when it is all gone. It is amazing how quickly all those little transactions add up. How does one keep track of it all? I definitely do not recommend turning teenagers loose with their own credit or debit cards without first teaching them what it means to empty their wallet and realize they don't have any more money and will have to wait to buy something else. They need to be taught to appreciate the value of money, comparing the cost of things. They need to see that four dollars spent on a cappuccino can also buy three two liter drinks, a gallon or so of gas, or four songs downloaded on their portable music device. They need to learn to question the value of what they are getting before handing over that hard-earned cash. They need to understand how long they have to work in order to afford the item they are getting ready to buy. They learn none of this if they have a parent-supported credit or debit card.

Our world is now fashioned for comfort and convenience. The advancements of technology and automation make it easy and affordable to obtain all the "toys" that didn't exist just a few generations ago. We want it now, since everyone else has one! We have to have it! Who wants to be the last person to try out the latest gadget? Unfortunately, our perceived social standing now requires us to maintain possessions at a certain level. I never knew sunglasses could be so expensive! I'm glad I don't wear them. Let's not even talk about shoes and clothes. A simple pair of socks can run you as much as $15 for a single pair. Who knew a logo could cost so much?

Retailers tell us to buy today and pay tomorrow. Besides, they won't charge us interest for six months! How nice of them. Remember that old saying that if a deal sounds too good to be true, it probably is? Unfortunately, most of us have fallen for the deal of the century—the power to charge! Put another way, this is the power to obtain something that you currently cannot afford. In exchange for this power, you are promising to pay more for the item than those who actually can afford it and pay for it with cash. In truth, these deals cost you more because of interest and other various types of fees.

Credit-card companies and banks are smart. They wouldn't be in business if they weren't. They know that if they can get you accustomed to using their card or get you on some revolving loan, you will eventually lose control and be unable to pay the entire balance at the end of the month to avoid paying finance charges. Interest rates and minimum payments are set to entice you to maintain a balance—a balance they hope will never go away. Once you have a balance, then you have a bill and an obligation on your part to pay that bill. Another bill means less cash available to spend on goods. Less cash means that you are more apt to use your charge card again. Once this vicious cycle is started, it is very hard to break. What's more, you have now added a level of complexity to your life that you did not have to deal with before you had a charge card. Life is complex enough without having to deal with the pressures of who charged what, when, where, and why. Someone once told me that he felt sorry for the charge card company because he avoided paying interest by paying his balance in full each month. He thought that in some twisted way, he was cheating them out of something and was afraid they would cancel his card because they never made any money off of him. In fact, he told me that on one particular month, he intentionally left a balance on his card just so the company could charge him interest! The sad fact is that the person who told me this was my dad.

What my father didn't realize is the credit card company or bank makes money for every single transaction made. Many do not realize that it's the retailer that has to pay when charge cards are used (usually 1-2% of the cost of the item), and they just pass that cost on to you in the form of higher prices. Many retailers are relying more and more of this form of payment to reduce the number of real employees they have to pay for. It really is funny how we develop a loyalty to these strange pieces of plastic. We even balk at other charge companies who dare try to get us to change over to their inferior card. Indeed, the war to get us to change seems to have escalated lately, based on the number of credit card solicitations sent in the mail each week. Well, let them solicit. We are the masters of our universe and we control what card we carry! But here's a question—who is the master and who is the slave?

Unless you have managed to maintain a simple lifestyle, most of us need a little help to keep track of our finances just to make sure we are not spending more than we make. There is simply too much detail to track in your mind. For those fortunate enough to be able to manage that aspect of your life well, you still might need some help planning for the future or for some of those big expenses that come around once a year. In either case, the *Budget Ninjas* process can help.

SOMETHING NEW

Starting something new can be a difficult and daunting task. When I was a young adult, I worked in a plastics factory on 3rd shift, feeding scrap plastic strips used for packaging into a grinder. It was a tough, sweaty job paying slightly more than minimum wage. The noise from the machine was deafening, probably the only thing keeping me awake. Each day was the same. Clock in, work, clock out. How did I end up here, and what was in store for my future? I really didn't care at that time, because I was young and naive with very few responsibilities, and I still lived with my parents. Sure, I could have made a career out of it, like my dad did in the machining business. Each week after I got my paycheck, I would go and blow the money almost as quickly as I got it. There was nothing to show for it, of course. Still, I thought to myself that this was a whole lot better than the job I had as a teenager on the dairy farm one summer where I was making a whole dollar an hour! Compared to dairy farming, I was living the dream. It is funny that I started my career in what most experts agree to be the worst job in the world (dairy farming) and now have a career in what most experts agree to be the best job in the world (working with computers). I guess I was a little motivated to do better and try something new, especially after getting rolled against a wall by a charging heifer trying to get out of the milking pen. Score: Cows 1, Dennis 0. As a friendly piece of advice to any farmers out there, don't try to get a cow to walk backwards through a stall. It doesn't work.

Since my dad was a blue-collar worker with four boys to feed and clothe, he had no money to send any of us to college, and although I loved to play just about every sport (I was extremely competitive and still remain so today), I wasn't good enough in any of them to get a scholarship. What I lacked in agility skills, however, I made up in academic skills. I made straight A's my senior year of high school. Home computers had just come out, and boy, did I love playing on them! Does anyone remember the old Atari 800 computers from the 80s (Sorry, Commodore 64 fans)? I considered myself pretty smart, graduating in the top five percent of my high school class. Why didn't I try for an academic scholarship? I don't know. None of my older brothers went to college. Nobody in my small town had applied for a scholarship before that I knew of, and I had no idea what I was doing.

I did make an attempt to get accepted into the United States Air Force Academy in Colorado Springs, Colorado. I made it through the interview process and even received a congressional nomination. The next step was to get a qualifying score on the SAT test that everyone had to take if they were going to college. Being a straight "A" student, I was hopeful that I would do well enough. I still remember the day of the test. It was held at Earlham College in Richmond, Indiana. The building was old and we were on the second floor. It was a pretty day and they had the windows open in the classroom. Halfway through the test, there was a constant irritating chirping noise coming from the window. Birds! More precisely, there was a dove sitting on the ledge. It was all I could do to concentrate on the English section of the test, and English was the subject that I struggled with the most. A few weeks after the test, I got the bad news that I had missed qualifying for the academy by only eight points! I had scored 99.36% of the total points needed to go to the Academy. Unfortunately, 99.36% was not good enough. The Academy granted no exceptions. My dreams of being an air force pilot faded quickly.

I don't regret not making it into the academy. After thinking about it, I would have landed smack dab in the middle of a couple of Gulf Wars if I had gone, and perhaps I would have been shot down. I'm thinking the dove was there for a reason.

Anyway, I graduated from high school and move down to South Carolina after my dad found a job there. So there I was, my first real job out of high school, working in a plastics factory.

No one ever told me that feeding long, thin strips of plastic into a high-powered shredding machine in the middle of the night was dangerous and not the best job in the world for me to start off on. It's much like working with those machines today that shred tree limbs and turn them into mulch. Little did I know that one evening, as I was feeding the beast, a piece of plastic wrapped itself around my arm. Of course, the machine grabbed the other end of the plastic strip and before I knew it, I saw smoke coming from my arm where the plastic was spinning around it at high speed, chewing away at my skin. Boy, was I lucky the machine didn't snap my arm off! It was at that very moment I decided I was going to find a way to go to college and work with computers, something for which I had a passion. I was definitely motivated to try something new! If you like the work you are doing, then it's not work, it's a career. Having a career in computers and number crunching and doing something that I love to do every day has been a blessing, and I have really enjoyed putting together this budgeting program and book. I'm really glad I tried something new. In an old western movie I love to watch, a young cowboy tells an older one that with a little risk, you can get big rewards. The seasoned cowboy looks at him and tells him that if the risk is little, the reward is little. Take some risks, try something new, and see what rewards are waiting for you!

Are you ready to try something new? Some studies suggest that you have to do something twenty-one days in a row to make it a habit. Do you think you could last that long on your first budget? It's not going to be that hard, and I believe you can do it. Take a little risk. What have you got to lose?

INSTANT GRATIFICATION

The anxiety that comes with financial stress is real, and it can actually make you sick. Stress by itself is not necessarily a bad thing. It's your body's natural reaction to protect you from danger. Stress is meant to heighten your senses and get you ready to take emergency action. Stress can actually save your life by pumping adrenaline into your body, giving you the strength to do something you wouldn't otherwise be able to do. I had my first adrenaline rush as a kid. I was playing by myself along the small river that ran outside our town. I was in a wooded area when I saw three other boys older than me who were always causing trouble. They spotted me and I heard one of them yell, "Let's get him!" Before I could even think, I was running like a wild gazelle through the woods and back to the main road. I was truly amazed at how fast I made it through, jumping logs, dodging trees, and plowing through brush like wild prey being pursued. I looked behind me, but the boys were nowhere in sight, and I made it back to town safe and sound. The stress-induced adrenaline played its part to protect me.

Financial stress is different. It's hard to get into "fight-or-flight" mode over unpaid bills. Who are you going to fight? Usually, the person you fight is the wrong target. Flight from your problems doesn't seem to work either, as there is nowhere to hide. Many are looking for the quick fix. They want instant gratification. They need instant relief for the financial pain they are experiencing. You may be under extreme pressure right now, either from your spouse or from someone to whom you owe money, to figure out how to come up with some quick cash. I can't promise that all your problems will disappear when you start a budget, but I will promise you that you will know what you can and can't do based on where you are today. Therefore, in a way, you will see instant results. You'll be able to answer those who are pressuring you. It may not be the answer they are looking for, but at least you'll have the information on hand to back up what you're saying. It's hard to argue with the cold hard facts. That's not to say you won't be challenged to come up with a different answer or to do something more dramatic than you were planning to do. But at least you'll have something to work from.

However, you don't want to get your relief from the wrong source. Marching down to Mr. Big's Payday Loans is an example of the wrong way to get relief from the financial stress you are experiencing. Mr. Big charges big interest and big fees, and if you don't pay back on time, he's got some big friends that are going to come visit you and give you a really big headache. Mr. Big will give you a "fix", but let me assure you, it's only temporary. Like a drug addict, you'll have to go back for more and more, and before you know it, you'll be way over your head and in deeper trouble. In the following weeks, I'll give you some better ideas for a way to come up with some quick money. In the meantime, what you need to do is get serious about preparing your first budget.

When dealing with creditors, you are in a much better negotiating position if you can tell them what you are prepared to do, even if it is not the full amount they are looking for, as opposed to telling them, "Sorry, I don't have the money to pay you." They are more likely to work with you when you can show them on paper that you are doing the best you can and will try your best to dig out of the hole you are in. Otherwise, you'll probably face a quick repossession or foreclosure, as well as potential legal trouble that will only make your financial situation worse. There's even a chance the creditor won't listen to you and continue to demand full payment. Remember, you are responsible for your debt. Since you are reading this book, my guess is that you want to do the right thing, make a better life for yourself and your family, and do everything you can not to repeat the same financial mistakes.

Just the act of preparing a budget will arm you with the ammunition you need to get started. You <u>will</u> get instant results. Your eyes will be opened to things you never thought were possible. To win the battle though, you'll need to work the budget as I describe in the rest of this book.

MOTIVATION

What's motivating you to try this new thing called a "budget"? What kind of instant gratification are you looking for? Newton had it right when he said, "Unless acted upon, a body at rest tends to stay at rest, and a body in motion tends to stay in motion." For many, my guess would be that your motivation comes from your spouse who has encouraged you to do something about the financial mess you all are in. If that's not the case, then there may be something you are looking for, perhaps a question that needs to be answered. The good news is that by virtue of having obtained this insightful book, you are now in motion and will tend to stay in motion until you find the answers you are looking for. So keep reading and don't lose that momentum!

People tackle problems in different ways. Some like to tackle the problem with guns blazing while others are more methodical, detailed, and systematic in their approach to problem solving. I've learned that when faced with financial problems, it's good to have a variety of perspectives on hand. Take for example a young couple who are getting ready to have their first child and want to finish the nursery. One of them, the husband, considers all the trivial details of everything that's going to be needed to get the nursery set up. He is already thinking about what each item is going to cost and the amount of work it's going to take to put everything together, and he starts laying out a detailed plan of how and when it can be done. The wife simply sees the finished room and what's going to be important for the next few years of their lives, and she is ready to negotiate and do without the non-essential parts of their lives. The husband is trying to maintain the lifestyle they currently have and is hard at work trying to fit in the cost of the nursery, calculating to the last detail when they will be able to obtain each item, and then preparing to tell his wife there are some things they can't afford. The visionary wife explains to her husband that the nursery is what's going to be important for the next few years of their lives. She then shares ideas for things they can do without instead of maintaining the lifestyle they currently have, and she negotiates on how to build the nursery as she sees it. You can see the advantage of having both perspectives on hand when dealing with large financial projects. There are many things in life I would have never considered to be a possibility if I hadn't first talked to my wife about it and listened to her perspective.

The same is true for those wanting to start a budget. I've had a career with computers most of my life, and in a way, I think much like a computer, sometimes getting lost in the details and losing sight of the big picture. In my mind, it all makes sense as I break down the problem into the smallest components and then tackle each one separately. The only problem is that there can be a lot of details when it comes to a budget. It's good to step back every now and then, look at the big picture, and make sure that you are on track to accomplish the goals you have set for yourself.

That's why I recommend for those of you who are married to make this a joint effort. One of you will most likely have the attention to detail that preparing a budget needs, and the other will probably have the oversight and vision to make sure you both stay on track. If done right, a budget can provide instant gratification to those who need answers now, and it can offer peace of mind for those who are detail-oriented by showing you that what you are promising can be achieved. The amount of detail that is generated from the use of bank cards can be huge, but most of us will continue to use them because of the convenience they bring us. That's why most people need a budget to help handle the detail and to allow them to focus on the goals they are trying to achieve.

THE DREADED QUESTION

What is a budget? No, that's not the question you are dreading. In the simplest terms, a budget is an itemized list of projected expenses over a given period of time compared to an itemized list of projected income over that same period. You could do a budget for a whole year, a month, a week, or even a day! Most families will do a budget for a month, because most bills come due once a month.

You may not realize it, but you are doing a budget in your head all the time. Let's say you are going shopping for some clothes. You set aside an amount of money that you want to spend, which is probably the amount of money you have in your pocket. As you shop, you try to keep as close as you can to the amount you wanted to spend. You may spend a little more or a little less, but that's ok as long as you have the money available. If you didn't spend as much as you thought, you then think to yourself, "I've got some money left over; what can I do with it?" A number of options start running through your head: you could get some coffee, buy some accessories, or even keep it in your pocket and save it for the next trip. Isn't it a great feeling to have some leftover money? What's left turns into "disposable income". Don't worry, you'll find a way to spend that money before it burns a hole in your pocket. I always do! Some thoughts that are most likely <u>not</u> going to make it into your brain, however, are "What's coming up that I could use this extra money for?" or "Maybe I should save this leftover money for a rainy day" or "I'll deposit this into my little piggy bank for Junior's college fund!" Few of us are trained to think along those lines because society as a whole no longer thinks this way. No one wants to take the time to think about whether or not their purchase is really worth the money it cost or what necessity of life they will have to do without later.

Take for example the cost of a pair of those really nice name-brand shoes. You know the ones I'm talking about. A good pair could set you back $200 or more. Now let's say your teen has a job making minimum wage and the only way they can get those shoes is to buy them with their own money. After taxes, they would have to work nearly two weeks to earn enough money to pay for those shoes. The sad truth is that most teens wouldn't even flinch at that thought and would gladly do it to maintain an acceptable social status (knowing they could probably do some heavy mooching off the parents while they save). I also realize the pressures of living in our social world and the need to keep up or be frowned upon. I can even see this social ranking to some extent in the adult world, especially in the practice known as "keeping up with the Joneses."

Now let's think about it from the other perspective. Let's say you spend a little too much on your clothes. You have more money in your bank account or pocket, though, so you don't think too much about it. A few options might possibly run through your head: you could decide to forgo the coffee or forget about the accessories. More likely, you give it no additional thought and continue on your merry way. I can't imagine very many people thinking, "Well, I've spent more money on clothes than I expected to, so let me see what kind of impact this will have on my future shopping opportunities." In fact, if I were to hear a teenager say that today, I think I would faint! I can almost guarantee that no one, as they were standing in line holding the item that was going to put them over the limit of what they wanted to spend, wondered whether or not they should put it back on the shelf and wait until additional funds were available. The only way that would happen is if cash were the only form of funds they had on hand!

It's easy to see the thought process that runs through your head when you go on a simple shopping trip. Now, how can you take that to the next level and put yourself in position to be able to shop for something on a larger scale, like a trip to some tropical paradise? It's hard to do that kind of math in your head. Many choose to do without the fun, the adventures and the sights this world has to offer simply because they do not take the time to plan ahead and prepare for the things that cost more than a week's wages. Instead, they elect to use the money they make on small, disposable items and rarely have anything to show for it.

If you've never been on a budget before, let me challenge you with a little test. Think back to the last time you got paid before your most recent paycheck. Now, can you tell me how much money you made and where it all went? Get out a piece of paper and start writing it down. Can you identify how you spent each dollar? Do you have anything solid to show for it or any money still left in the bank? My guess is that the total expenses you can account for will not even come close to what you brought home. So, <u>where did it all go</u>? This is the question most dread the most, and it's frustrating because on the surface, it seems like it should be a very easy question to answer. That's where the trouble starts, however. When acceptable responses are not received in a timely manner to such a simple and innocent question, there's a good chance major trouble is getting ready to break loose. The fact that you are not able to answer suggests you might be trying to hide something. Your spouse might think that maybe you bought something for yourself without giving any thought to him or her. Perhaps you went out with your friends at lunch and forgot to tell your spouse. Perhaps you don't even remember! You respond in anger because you know in your heart you don't have anything of value to show for it, so it must be your spouse's fault, not yours! Frustration grows on both sides. Each of you begins to mistrust and lose respect for the other. You might even take it to the next level and keep your money separate (assuming both of you are earning an income). That move makes the situation worse because you then begin to fight over who should pay for what and how the other is not doing his or her fair share. You can see how serious a problem this can be. This question, or better yet, the inability to answer this question, is one of the main reasons for divorces today.

I'm not saying the "Where did it all go?" question is a bad question to ask. It's a valid question that deserves attention and serious contemplation, especially if you want to avoid the fight that will occur the next time the question is asked. It definitely should not be ignored. If you are unable to answer the question successfully, your best strategy is to simply tell the truth, that you don't know. However, making a blanket statement like that will do you no good unless you combine it with a promise of action, demonstrating your commitment to answer the question correctly next time. The action you will take is, of course, establishing a budget.

TRIVIAL MATTERS

Our minds are not inclined to keep track of every little financial transaction we make throughout the week or month. We were created with both short-term and long-term memory. The memory of purchasing a small disposable item falls into the short-term memory category. The memories of that purchase will quickly fade within a day or two. It's too bad our noodles didn't come equipped with an automatic nightly backup (computer geek talk) of short-term memory. Short term memory is powerful, detailed, and precise, able to store all kinds of trivial data, but it only lasts a few fleeting hours or days. After that, the details become vague until they eventually fade away. Think about all your five senses—smelling, touching, hearing, seeing, and tasting. These are all avenues for data to enter your mind. Think about how crazy you would go if you were able to recall every touch, every smell, every sound, every taste, and every place you went in the last twenty-four hours. You would go nuts! You wouldn't be able to focus. That's why paper was invented, so you can record the important details for historical purposes. And that's what a budget is for, to record a detailed history of what you have done with your money.

No reasonable person should expect you to remember every detail about every purchase, but with a budget, it is possible. With my budgeting techniques, I'll show you how to keep the amount of detail down to a minimum in order to make budgeting as easy as it can be. For example, I will explain to you how you can use a simple envelope system to reduce the amount of detail you have to deal with. Some would say all you really need is an envelope system instead of a budget. True, for very simple budgets that don't require planning for the future, capturing trends, and answering all those "what if" questions, an envelope system might work. With today's lifestyles, however, nothing is ever simple anymore, and you'll get limited benefit from only using envelopes.

Doing a monthly budget is really no more difficult than planning to go shopping. The first time you do a budget, the process may take longer because you have to think about everyone you need to pay. But after that, you have a written record from the prior month, and it is very easy to move on from there.

As you can see, a budget is a simple tool you can use to obtain answers to your most common financial questions. However, I think many budgets fall short by only listing income and expenses. You'll get some answers by doing that, and those are very important steps, but there is so much more valuable information you are missing out on by not taking your budget to the next level with a few additional steps. There is a difference between creating a budget and working a budget. A budget is a tool that must be used and worked, not just created and reviewed once a month. Suppose you plant a vegetable garden. You work the soil, add fertilizer and other organic material, and you then carefully plant your seed. Are you done? By doing nothing else, you could watch your garden grow, but a thousand weeds will grow alongside your sprouts. By the end of the month, it will be very difficult to tell the difference between the weeds and the vegetables. A better idea is to work your garden throughout the month, taking care of the weeds as they crop up. You'll want to do the same with your budget, working it as financial weeds start popping up throughout the month.

The budget you create with *Budget Ninjas* is a living document, not something you do only at the beginning of the month. If you stopped there, we would have to assume the rest of your month is going to go exactly as you had planned. That will never happen, which is why you use the *Budget Ninjas* budget throughout the month to answer your questions as your life unfolds. It comes alive and speaks volumes, preventing arguments from breaking out. If an argument concerning finances does erupt, your budget will quickly point out where the problems are and a quick resolution can be implemented.

Simplicity is the answer. If you have to worry about too much detail, you will never stay on budget. If the budget doesn't give you real answers to real questions, what good is it? That's why I set out to develop my own approach to budgeting—one that is simple, straightforward, easy to maintain, easy to explain, and easy on time.

A budget should be flexible, able to adjust to your lifestyle. The biggest misconception that many people have with budgets is that everything must be exact down to the penny. Not true. I'll show you how you can use nice round numbers, not only in your budget but also when paying your bills. Some might say, "It's too restrictive and there is too much detail to keep up with." Again, not true. This budget gives you freedom to know what you can safely spend on items you would otherwise be too afraid to purchase. As far as detail goes, you need only be concerned with the detail that affects your checkbook. Other budget programs might have you itemize exactly how much you grossed, deduct how much went to taxes, insurance, FICA, etc. However, you need to see only what goes into and what comes out of your checkbook. You will wonder why you never had a budget before when you see how easy it can be.

So how does one go about putting together a budget? I know many of you are chomping at the bit, ready to get started. However, we still have a few more things to cover first.

ALERT! ALERT!

Before we go any further, heed this warning: DO NOT LET YOUR BUDGET RUN YOUR LIFE! For those of you just starting out, it's very easy to allow your budget to dictate how you and your family are going to live. You could end up turning yourself and your family into living robots. You would be preprogrammed for the whole month with instructions on what you could and could not do, controlled by the budget program. What kind of life is that? Of course, this will not sit well with the family and they will let you know quickly and often how the word "budget" has turned into a nasty curse word. Seriously, even if you are in debt reduction mode or are under serious financial strain, do not clamp down so hard that no one can breathe. A budget does give you serious power, and in the wrong hands, it could be used in a very controlling manner. Just ask Congress! I'm not sure which is worse, not being able to answer the question "Where did all the money go?" or having to live with the consequences of constant saying, "Sorry, that's not in the budget!" Don't turn into a budget dictator. Spare yourself some serious heartburn and heartache. There has to be some balance. That's why I love my wife so much! She truly is the "better half" of our marriage. She brings me the balance I need, telling me when I am getting a little too out of control (or I should say too controlling) and when I need to loosen up. If you are married, listen to what your spouse is trying to tell you. Seek out their perspective, and do not take offense when you receive criticism on your approach to budgeting. You may have the right motives for managing the family finances better, but your spouse and kids are not little robots to be programmed and ordered around.

Another potential side effect of living on a budget is the possibility of becoming a major cheapskate, a miserly, stingy person who tries to avoid paying a fair share of costs or expenses. I believe that if I were not a married man and were left to my own devices, I would be a major cheapskate. Look for some of these warning signs a few months after living on a budget to see if you might be becoming one. Using the chart below in Figure 1-2, add up the total points you scored to see how well you did.

A few signs you might be a cheapskate (add 1 point for each occurrence):

1. You use the term "It's not in the budget" (1 point per occurrence)
2. You constantly question other family members' spending decisions
3. You don't do necessary repairs on your house or car
4. You won't go to the doctor to get necessary prescription medicine and instead try to "doctor" the family yourself
5. You avoid giving to charity.
6. You won't buy popcorn and peanuts for your kids at the old ball game or the movies
7. You allow others to buy your meal but never return the favor
8. You take the time to calculate how much tip you leave for a dinner out just to make sure you don't leave "too much." Add another point if you "round down" to the nearest dollar, instead of rounding up.
9. You encourage others to do any of the above
10. Someone you love has called you a penny-pinching miser

FIGURE 1-2

How did you score? Did you score less than three? Good! Keep in mind that this is just a partial list. I would say even if you got only one point, you might want to ask someone you love and trust whether they think you are becoming a cheapskate. The sad fact is I have scored a point for every one of these warning signs at one time or another in my life. For those who were already a cheapskate before they bought this book (which I doubt they would have spared the money for), this mindset can be extremely difficult to overcome. If it makes you feel better, I still struggle with stinginess today, and many times I have to force myself to freely give. That's where the rubber meets the road for many. Giving is extremely hard to do when you are trying to achieve a financial goal through your budget. You have to have faith that it's all going to work out in the end, and you can't sweat the small stuff. It's not worth it.

You could almost say that a penny-pinching miser has put their faith in their money and in their ability to get more. That's why they protect their wealth so fiercely and put so much value on controlling it. To them, money is the complete answer to their problems. It's easy to fall into this mindset because in today's society, money is power. With the right amount of money, you have the power to do just about anything. However, never turn your passion for living on a budget into a love and desire for more money. The love of money is the root of all kinds of evil. If you start feeling as though you are putting your trust and faith in the almighty dollar bill, just flip it over to the back side and read what's above the center "one". That will help you restore focus.

Don't end up like the penny-pinching miser everyone avoids like the plague. The friends you are hounding to pay you back the few bucks you lent them for lunch are the same ones you'll need when you lose your job because of your nasty disposition, when there is some natural disaster, or when the political landscape really starts to heat up. Take a turn and bring in those donuts to work, and then share them! I know that's extremely hard for those with a sweet tooth, like me. Most likely, you won't have any true friends if you consistently live the ways of a miser. I love the words of Clarence, who wrote, "No man is a failure who has friends." Most of you know this quote from the famous movie *It's a Wonderful Life.* You feel sorry for poor George Bailey. You can tell he wasn't one who lived on a budget. He was always trying to help his friends and neighbors make it through to the next day. When it came down to his desperate need for quick cash, he had no reserves, just a life insurance policy with very little equity. But he didn't need it. All he needed (although he didn't know it until the last minute) was the value of a couple hundred friends! Keep in mind the budget is only a tool, a means to an end. There are always other ways to make ends meet. Do not live your life through the narrow lens of a budget. You'll make life miserable for yourself and for all those around you. Take it one day at a time. Each day has its own troubles to worry about.

So, what is the right balance between being a penny-pinching miser and a free-spender? The answer depends on your particular situation. It would be rare that you would need to lean to one extreme or the other. If you have creditors knocking on your door or threatening to come take away your only source of transportation, you might need to temporarily go into extreme budgeting mode, but only after getting an opinion from all family members impacted by the decision and agreeing unanimously that this is the best, and perhaps only, path forward. Just keep in mind that you'll be lucky to make it through a whole month in extreme mode before the rest of the family needs a break. Make sure you give them that break during the next month; otherwise, you risk "breaking" your marriage! If you are the person controlling the budget, you might decide to sacrifice your own wants and desires (again, temporarily—see previous cheapskate warning signs) just to give other family members some breathing room. You might need to be creative as you accomplish your goals. In *Week 5 - My Income,* I will give you some ideas for generating some additional funds.

What about the other extreme of not using a budget at all and throwing caution to the wind? What if you won the lottery? Is it smooth sailing after that? You can do a simple Internet search for past lottery winners to see that most of their lives were ruined shortly after winning, sometimes even to the point of death. What happened? Some had marriages that failed, some gambled away all their winnings, some had to go into hiding to keep their fortunes safe, and some simply met a tragic end. My guess is that they experienced a quick and complete loss of balance in their lives, wreaking havoc and upsetting everything they thought they knew about life. Having the riches of a king doesn't necessarily make your life rich. You could end up lonelier than the penny-pinching miser. Sure, you'll have plenty of false friends who hang around looking for a free ride, but are these folks willing to lay down their lives for you? Would you have the mindset to do the same for them if you were put in such a position? What if the world's economy suddenly came to a screeching halt and all your money became worthless? Would these folks have your back? Better to be prepared than to be caught off-guard and let some event throw your life into turmoil.

LAST BIT OF ADVICE

For a family, a budget requires teamwork and communication. Lack of communication concerning finances is probably the number one reason couples get into arguments to begin with. There can be no secrets. Lay it all on the table. Show each other your pay-stubs. Fess up to your bad spending habits. Be prepared to act like a duck and let the criticism roll off your back. Then agree to work together for the common good and to share in the rewards for your efforts—and there will be rewards!

PURPOSE

I promised to share with you at the end of this week how to get off this crazy merry-go-round of pursuing "things" and to share a few tips on how to live a happy, content life. It all comes down to purpose. What is your purpose in this life? That's the age-old question that everyone tries to answer for themselves at some point or another during their life. "Why was I put here on earth?" You know the answer. It's the answer you gave as a child, or at least thought, when your mother, father, or teacher would ask you, "What do you want to be when you grow up?" What gifts and talents do you have that the rest of the world needs? Every one of us is a unique creation. There's no one like you. You know deep down what makes you tick. All you have to do is finish this sentence: "I'm happiest when…" Are you happiest when serving

25

others? Do you love to research? Are you good at communicating? Do you love to organize things? If you've never had a heart-to-heart with yourself and answered this question in your mind, think about it seriously for a while. Ask those who are closest to you what they think. You'll know you are on the right track when that thing you love to do begins to bear fruit. I'm not talking about literal fruit, like apples and oranges. I'm talking about the fruit of your labors. Once you have that figured out, use the budget program outlined in this book to help you achieve your dreams and purpose in this life.

Your career may have nothing to do with your purpose except providing a means for you to achieve it. With many, it can be difficult to distinguish between career and purpose because the majority of your waking hours are spent getting ready for work, working, and resting from your work. When do you have any time to focus on anything else? I can tell you, though, that it is almost impossible to stop a person who truly understands their purpose. A purpose-driven individual is also an extremely resourceful individual and will discover power beyond their own abilities, allowing them to fulfill their dreams. Over a decade ago, I was driven to finish my first budgeting book and software that would offer an easy way to manage a budget. I had no idea how to write and publish a book and no experience writing software for a personal computer, as all my prior experience was writing software for mainframe systems. However, I knew my purpose and I knew what I had to accomplish. I was driven. At the time, my two children were very young. I would take my kids to McDonalds, and while they were crawling through the tunnels in play land, I was developing a comprehensive searchable help system for my software. It was an exhilarating experience as I got closer and closer to achieving my goal. It took several months to complete, but they seemed like days. There is nothing truer than the old saying, "Time flies when you're having fun."

Your purpose may change over time, and you may go through many different seasons. As you explore and define your purpose, though, try not to worry so much about money. As I stated in the beginning, the purpose of this budget is not to get you focused on your finances, but to get you into a position in which you don't have to. That's what living is all about.

WEEK 1 – QUESTIONS & DISCUSSION
(You may copy this page as needed)

1. What is a budget?

    _____

    _____

    _____

2. What types of budget programs have you used in the past?

    _____

    _____

    _____

3. If you've been on a budget before, why did you stop budgeting?

    _____

    _____

    _____

4. TRUE or FALSE
    Credit card companies do not make any money if you pay your balance in full each month.

5. What question are you looking to answer by getting on a budget?

    _____

    _____

    _____

6. What would you do if you won the lottery?

    _____

    _____

    _____

7. TRUE or FALSE
    For a family, only the detailed person needs to be involved when creating the budget. The other person would just mess it up.

WEEK 2 - UNCONVENTIONAL WEAPONS

Now that we've gone through all the deep material, it's time to start equipping you with the weapons and tools you'll need to defeat your financial enemies. These are not the weapons you would ordinarily use when going into battle, since most of the time, the battles you wage will be against yourself and your own mind. Some of these weapons you may already be familiar with, but you have no idea how much power they can give you or how much damage they can cause if misused. Like a true ninja, you'll need to master these weapons in order to become a skilled budget master ninja.

PATIENCE

"Patience is a virtue" is a very well-known saying that many of us have grown up hearing time after time, usually after our own displays of impatience. Indeed, patience is an extremely powerful weapon that can help you in many ways. As you take the time to build your budget, you are going to need patience to uncover all your bills and the details of when they need to be paid. You'll need patience with your family as they adjust to this new way of managing money. You'll need patience as you work month after month to achieve your goals and dreams. The trouble is that nobody likes to wait. For example, let's say you go to an amusement park and get in line for a popular ride. What do you have to do? You have to wait. You have to have patience if you want to experience the thrills of what the ride has to offer. As you get closer to the front of the line, your heart begins to pump faster in anticipation of the thrill to come. There is an art to patience. Enjoy the process. Feel the rush as you take another step closer. Sometimes the excitement comes from not knowing what it is going to be like once you get there. Learn to enjoy the ride before you even climb aboard! Learn patience, and once you make it to the front of the budget line, you'll be shocked to discover how much is waiting for you.

Financially speaking, patience is one of the most powerful forces in money management. That power can be demonstrated, for instance, through compound interest. Although you won't need to master the concept of interest in this book, I do want to demonstrate its power. Suppose an 18 year-old gets his first job and says he is going to save one dollar a day until he retires. He faithfully stuffs his dollar bill in a rusty coffee can each day. On his birthday at the ripe age of sixty-seven, he opens his cans and counts what he has saved. He pulls out nearly $18,000! That's a decent retirement fund, but could he have done better? Let's say he instead takes his dollar bills and invests them in a conservative account that yields a 7% annual return. When he retires at age sixty-seven, he will pull nearly $146,000 from his savings! That's eighteen times as much as he made stuffing it into a can. That's the magic of compound interest over a long period of time. If you are young, start investing now and watch your fortune grow as you get older and older. It doesn't take a lot of money to make a lot of money if you have time on your side.

PERSISTENCE

When my son was taking a karate class, I noticed a sign posted on the wall that read, "A black belt is simply a white belt that refused to give up." With time, dedication, and a little hard work, anyone can be a black belt. All it takes is persistence, whether in martial arts or money. Don't see your finances as a mess that's impossible to correct. You may be a budget white belt now, but you can build on what you have, completing one goal after another, as long as you refuse to give up. Figuring out how you are going to make ends meet may appear to be an impossible task, but it can be made easy if you remain persistent and diligent. Several million years ago, there was no Grand Canyon. What started out as a small creek turned into the Colorado River. Over millions of years, the river cut into the earth, carving a canyon over 277 miles long, several miles wide, and sometimes over a mile deep. That's the effect nature can have when persistence is combined with patience. What kind of effect can you have on your finances when you do the same?

DILIGENCE

"If it is to be, it is up to me." Remember those ten catchy two-letter words. I learned those words from a mentor with whom I worked when I was young. Whatever it is you are trying to achieve; you will be playing the starring role. You can't sit back and do nothing, expect others to do it for you, or do something repeatedly and expect everything to work itself out. I'm sure you have heard before that the definition of insanity is doing the same thing over and over and expecting different results. You can't live life as you have been and expect everything to fix itself. Have a little faith in yourself and your unique abilities. See yourself in the financial position you desire, and then be diligent in working toward that end.

You can create all the financial goals you want and have all the faith in the world that they can be achieved. However, it you don't put some action behind those goals and take diligent steps to see them come to pass, you'll find yourself empty-handed and discouraged. Combine diligence with patience and persistence, and you have a solid formula for tackling any issue that comes your way, financial or otherwise.

SELF-CONTROL

One of the hardest weapons for a budget ninja to master is self-control. Many people have a difficult time with self-control, especially when they are involved in an emotionally charged event. Road rage is a common example, as something as trivial as driving the speed limit can cause those behind you to boil with rage, swerving back and forth as though they are ready to mow you over if you don't get out of the way. Your ability to make good decisions is impaired when you have lost self-control, and if you are put in a position in which you have to make a financial decision without this weapon, chances are you will make the wrong decision.

Losing control can cost you financially, but worse, it means someone else has gained control over you. Friends and family can easily influence you to do something you wouldn't normally do if you were left to your own devices. If you allow this to happen, you have lost a measure of self-control. You are letting others guide your actions and decisions. Around the holidays, for example, everyone is out shopping and spending and having a good time and you want to do the same. There's nothing wrong with doing so; you just need to choose which activities you engage in based on logic and reason, not emotion or what others are doing. After all, the holidays can take a tremendous toll on the family budget. It is so easy these days to make your purchases online and charge those purchases. When you charge to your credit card, it's hard to see the impact that decision is going to have on your future finances. Those who purchase with a credit card are more likely to spend a greater amount than those who pay in cash or with their debit card.

Even when you believe you are in solid control of your budget and your finances, remember not to exert too much control as described in the previous week. Overusing an otherwise good trait can be almost as bad as or worse than underusing that trait.

Choose to be a leader and not a follower. Leaders are always in control. They should listen to the advice and counsel of those around them, but they make their decisions based on experience, sound counsel, and the direction in which they want to go. Thus, it makes sense that in order to be a leader, you have to know where you are going. Throughout this book, I'll be teaching you how to be a leader, because you will be learning where you want to go and how you are going to get there.

AGILITY

I wish I could give you the assurance that once you start the budgeting process, everything is going to go perfectly and all will be well with the world. Unfortunately, there will be bumps in the road. You'll sometimes need to react quickly to your changing financial position when the unexpected happens. That means not waiting until the end of the month to see how it all unfolds. Take the bull by the horns and take care of business. By reacting early, you can make arrangements to reduce the impact of the unbudgeted expense by moving a purchase to a later month, reducing another expense, or trying to find some additional income.

There may also be opportunities you run across that require a quick decision. You'll be in a better position to make a quality decision if you stay on top of your budget and know what you have left to work with for the month. You may not have time to go home and pull up your budget on the computer to see where you stand. You might need to make a decision right then and there. Keeping the status of your budget fresh in your mind can be very helpful.

JOY

The last weapon that I believe is a must-have in your arsenal is a measure of joy and happiness. If you walk around all defeated, you'll be looking for any excuse to call it quits. As long as you have air in your lungs, put a smile on your face. Make sure you take time to celebrate your achievements. There's nothing good that can come from maintaining a sour disposition. People will avoid you, you'll miss out on opportunities, and it could even impact your chances for a promotion at work. Just because you are struggling financially doesn't mean you can't enjoy life and what it has to offer.

YOUR TOOLBOX

We've talked about the weapons you'll need to successfully build and work a budget, but what about the tools you'll need? When building something, you need tools and supplies. What supplies will you need and how are you going to use them?

I recently had my roof replaced due to hail damage. Can you imagine how long it would have taken the working crew to put up all those shingles if they had to physically nail every shingle in place with a hammer? It can be done, but the right tool for that job is a nail gun. I can see how frustration can easily set in if you don't have the right tool for the job. In my kitchen, the faucet is always working its way loose. The only problem is I do not have a wrench long enough to reach in through the back side of the sink to tighten it down. Also, I once noticed the steps leading down into my swimming pool were becoming slightly stained. I went out there and scrubbed and scrubbed for months. It helped a little, but it didn't look shiny and white as I wanted it to. One day, I went to the pool store for some supplies and asked the lady if there was anything that could be done about my steps. She pointed out a bottle of liquid chemicals of some sort and told me to pour a little of those chemicals on my steps and watch the stains dissolve away. I was skeptical, as I had spent hours painfully scrubbing with little to show for my effort. However, I took the liquid home and eagerly went to the pool steps to pour it out. Then I sat and watched for a few minutes. Nothing, just as I had figured. But then, all of a sudden, the stains started lifting away like a thin sheet of paper. It was like magic! I was so excited to have found something that actually worked, and worked better than my hardest scrubbing. What a relief. Then, however, I started to question myself. Why did I wait so long before asking the professionals who do this for a living? The answer, unfortunately, was my own arrogance and stubbornness, arrogance for thinking that nothing could clean the steps as well as I could, and stubbornness for not being willing to consider that there might possibly be a better solution. Sometimes, I am my own worst enemy. I just needed the right tool for the job.

The same goes for your budget. While for some, a pencil and a piece of paper may be all that's needed, others may need more advanced tools to help them gain control. If you don't have the right tools to help, the job can be more difficult than it really needs to be. What are the ingredients and tools needed to build your budget? I'll devote a separate week to each key ingredient. The good news is you have already read about the first key ingredient in week one:

1. You. Somebody has to do the dirty work and that person is you. If you are married, your spouse should also be available to participate and work with you as you build your budget. Review Week 1 often to keep everything in proper perspective.

2. Your checkbook. To be more specific, you will need a balanced checkbook. This may seem like such a trivial chore, and with instant access to your account through the Internet via your computer or smart phone, why bother? This week will tell you why!

3. Your goals. I'm sure getting out of debt is most people's Reason Number One for starting a budget. What's yours? We'll talk about the difference between financially driven goals and purpose driven goals.

4. Your income. Hopefully, you have got some money to work with, and whether it is a steady job, retirement savings, or part-time work, we'll talk about what's needed to get the job done and some easy ways to make more income.

5. Your bills. This is one of the more difficult ingredients to pull together. It sounds easy on the surface, but you will be shocked to see how many bills you actually pay in a given month. We'll talk about ways to cut some of those bills down.

6. Your budget. By this time, you'll be ready to mix all your ingredients together to establish your budget. You'll decide whether to use paper or a computer. You'll learn how to avoid cash flow problems, how to work your budget during the month and make it work for you, and how to prepare for the next month. You'll learn how to read your budget to answer the questions you've always wanted answered.

Now let's get to work figuring out how to put your budget together!

WEEK 2 – QUESTIONS & DISCUSSION
(You may copy this page as needed)

1. Share an example where demonstrating patience saved you money.

   _____

   _____

   _____

2. Share an example where a lack of patience cost you money.

   _____

   _____

   _____

3. Finish this sentence: "If it is to be..."

   _____

4. TRUE or FALSE.
   When shopping, always use a credit card so you can earn points and rewards.

5. Which unconventional weapon of budgeting would you consider most important, and why?

   _____

   _____

   _____

6. Name some of the tools you'll need to prepare your budget.

   _____

   _____

   _____

WEEK 3 - MY CHECKBOOK

Let's start with your checkbook. Is it balanced? Is the word "balanced" even a part of your financial vocabulary? The budget process I will be taking you through will work best if you know how much money you have in your checking account to begin with, and the only way to know that is to keep your checkbook balanced. When you balance your checkbook successfully, it simply means that you and the bank are in agreement with the amount of money they say you have in your bank account. You agree that what they say you have available to spend is correct. If you do nothing, the bank is always correct regardless of whether or not they actually are. I'm guessing you're not married to the bank, so I wouldn't put so much trust in them. They have thousands, perhaps even millions of customers, so who are you to them? They are not interested in your feelings. When you tell them you "feel" like they made a mistake and you should have more money in the bank, you're not going to get very far without some facts to back up your accusations. The following lists several reasons why you will want to balance your checkbook each month.

SIX REASONS TO BALANCE YOUR CHECKBOOK

REASON 1 – BANK ERRORS

I love that Monopoly game card that reads, "Bank error in your favor, collect $200." In all my life, I have never had a bank error in my favor. I have never had the teller machine spit out an extra ten or twenty. I have never had a stranger accidentally use my account number when making a huge deposit or even a small deposit for that matter. Am I the only one so unlucky? Unfortunately, it is usually the other way around. "Bank error not in your favor, pay $200." You look at your bank statement and wonder where all those charges came from. When you get your monthly bank statement, don't blindly trust that everything they have recorded is accurate. Trust me, after writing hundreds of computer programs, I know how easy it is to make a mistake in the code. Computers are very finicky machines, and they do only as they are told. Many programs contain thousands of lines of code, so the chances that there is a mistake somewhere are pretty high. You've heard the stories in the news: a couple receives a phone bill for three hundred billion dollars! Banking software is no different. In fact, the number of lines of code for such complex programming is astronomical.

What's worse, it may take months or years before the right set of variables is present for the computer bug to rear its ugly head and deduct

35

more money than it should have from your account. I've seen this firsthand in many programs I have written (none that deducted money from some poor unsuspecting soul, fortunately). You test and test, work with the people who will use the application, have them test, and get them to sign off on it, saying it looks good to them. Then, many months later, the right set of circumstances are combined to cause your program to report inaccurate results. It's a common issue in the computer programming industry. Programmers are only human, and there is only so much time to get the job done and so many test cases to go through, so they can't catch everything. When you use your bank card, that particular transaction has to go through several companies and systems before it hits your account. It may look instantaneous to you because those transactions are travelling at the speed of light, but the more systems your transaction has to travel through, the higher the chances an error may occur. Also, banks employ hordes of imperfect humans who are prone to make a ton of clerical errors. If that doesn't send shivers up your spine, I don't know what will! Bank errors are an important reason for you to balance your checkbook, just to keep them honest.

REASON 2 – IDENTIFY FRAUD

Another reason you will want to balance your checkbook is to make sure you are not the victim of identity fraud. Identity fraud can occur in many different forms. I'll highlight a few areas of concern.

The bank may not have made a mistake, but somehow, someone got hold of your account information and started spending your money like a drunken sailor. It's a major problem today, especially with the economy in such bad shape.

As a prior Information Technology (IT) manager, I know a vast number of ways that can be used to access personal data about you, as well as how to use that information to gain access to your assets. Each year, the company I work for performs an annual security assessment. We actually hire the "bad guys" (professional hackers) to come in and try to hack into our networks, our systems, our websites, and our building to see what they can discover and how far in they can get. A variety of methods are used, including socially engineered techniques that attempt to manipulate people into freely giving personal information about someone. These "bad guys" are good, and they guarantee they will succeed in getting access to information they have no business seeing.

One of the most popular techniques is called spoofing. If you are being spoofed, someone is pretending to be you to get access to information that typically only you would have access to. There are a number of ways to do this, including email spoofing and caller ID spoofing. When hackers email spoof, they send out an email that appears to be from you. The recipient, which could be either a person or a business, may be tricked into thinking it is you and give out account information about you, or worse, allow the hackers to change the password to your accounts. I was really sad when I recently received an email from someone in my company who had passed away a few years ago. Either ghosts are real, or spoofing is taking place! When you receive an email from someone you know and it has a suspicious link in it, do not click on the link.

With caller ID spoofing, it is fairly easy to trick the phone system to send a different number than the actual phone number being used. Large companies encounter this problem often. The help desk receives a call that appears to be from a person who works for the company, and the caller asks them to reset their password because they forgot it. The help desk sees the call is from an internal number, assumes it is a legitimate call, and resets the password. Since most company wireless networks extend well beyond the four walls of the company building, it is very easy for the hacker to sit in the parking lot, access the network, and use their new passwords to access email, applications, and more. Many folks use their company email accounts to hold on to sensitive and secure data about their personal accounts, so it is easy to gain access to bank information, credit card information, and more. Also, since the hacker now has access to your email account, he can easily proceed with email spoofing and do more damage.

Ask your company if they do an annual security assessment. If they don't, be very careful with the personal information that you store in your company email account! Based on the statistics I have read; no company is 100% secure. In fact, it is common to find major security holes that remain year after year because it is too expensive to upgrade systems to protect everything. Hacking techniques are also becoming more sophisticated, and some hackers even receive sponsorship from foreign government agencies. Many hackers are well funded and work to improve their skills, just as any other professional would. In the past two years alone, I have been informed by my state, my employer, and by my hospital that there was a chance that personal information about me could have been stolen and used for identity fraud. Sure, they offered free credit reports and identity theft monitoring services, but those services are limited in what they can do to prevent identity theft. Luckily, I have been spared so far (knock on wood).

If a drug addict in desperate need of a fix has access to your social security number, pin or date of birth, you also are not in a good situation. I should know because at one time, I had a relative who was a drug addict and would say or do anything to get the next hit. It's a terrible disease, one of those few that society tries to avoid and pretend isn't there in order to avoid the illegal activities and social stigma of those inflicted with it. Because these folks are shunned by society, they don't get the treatment they need, and the disease becomes worse and worse until it destroys their lives and the lives of those around them. It's the leprosy of the modern era. Other diseases get sympathy, sponsors for fundraising events, and funding from the government in support of the attempt to find a cure, but not so much with drug addicts. I have found through conversations with many of my friends that a drug addict can usually be found somewhere in everyone's family tree. Your own finances could be suffering right now from the addiction of someone you know. Be careful, then, with the personal information you give to family and friends. You may want to perform your own personal security assessment.

Another common way to become an identify fraud victim is through the web sites you visit and emails you open. The exposure you have online is tremendous, as there are many unscrupulous individuals around the world who don't speak your language but are becoming very creative in finding ways to trick you out of personal information. It doesn't take much to be tricked. It's easy to send emails that appear to be from your bank, asking you to click on a link to view details about a particular "problem" they have detected on your account. They even go so far as to create their own web site that looks like your bank account's site. You follow the link to their phony site, enter your information and password, and BOOM! They have access to your account, and you're a victim of identity fraud. Never click on a link to a financial site. Instead, always enter the website address yourself, typing it from memory, or go to the site from your favorites, not from the link they are showing you in the email. The best advice I can give you is to get a separate computer that is used only for your personal finances, visiting sites you already know are safe. You should not let anyone else use it for checking email, surfing, social sites, or games. It's your computer and its only use is for paying bills online, purchasing, checking accounts, and using your budgeting software. This computer should also have up-to-date antivirus software installed. You really need that software on all your computers, but it is a must-have on the computer you use to handle your finances.

Many people are using another trick to get your name on a spam list. They send bulk emails to random computer-generated email addresses asking you if you are interested in something. They nicely provide a link for you to be "removed" or "unsubscribed" from their email list if you are not interested. Guess what you have done when you click the link to unsubscribe? You have just validated and informed that company (or individual) that you are a real person with a valid email address. Now they will record your email address as valid and then sell it to many companies around the world who are looking for addresses of possible consumers. Before you know it, you are being spammed to death. You click more links to be removed from the mailing lists, but that only makes the problem worse. I'm not saying that all emails are of ill intent. However, many of the spam emails you get may ask for personal information in order to try and steal your identity. The best strategy for dealing with questionable messages is not to click the link to be removed from their email list, but rather to forward such unwanted emails to your email provider's spam list. If you are not sure what the email address of the spam list is, ask your Internet or email provider for it.

Keeping on the theme of identity theft, be careful with the information you give to anyone who calls you on the phone. They may have just enough personal information about you to get you to believe they are a bank employee calling to resolve a discrepancy in your account. It is very easy to get your hands on this kind of information if the victim banks with one of the larger institutions. The thieves will call random phone numbers, and eventually they will find someone who banks with the large institution they are pretending to work with. Therefore, you should never believe anyone who calls you directly. It's rare for a financial institution to call you; they are more likely to send you mail detailing the issue and asking you to call them. If you get such a call, ask for the caller's full name, address, and phone number. If they don't give it to you, hang up. If they do give you the information, tell them you will call back and then hang up. Look up the main customer service number of the bank, either with a phone book or through the Internet. Then call that number and give the customer service representative the information you recorded from the previous caller. Have them verify that the call was legitimate and then try to resolve whatever issue it is. But be careful; an identity thief will have a variety of tricks to distract you while you are on the phone, and before you know it, you may have given him enough information to access your account. I get these types of strange calls at least once a week. It's usually a recording stating that there is nothing wrong with your credit card account, but they need to discuss a particular issue. They then proceed to ask you to press a number to connect with a so-called operator. Don't do it! It is a scam.

One of my friends had a unique suggestion to make it easier to discover when you are being victimized through your credit cards and bank cards. When you go out to dinner and you are ready to leave a tip, make the total end in the same number every time. Let's say the number you like is 76. In that case, one night you might pay $25.76 including tip, and another night you might pay $17.76 including tip. Notice that the amount always ends with a 76. I believe this is valuable advice, because a restaurant is one of the few places where you hand over your credit card to a complete stranger and they walk away to do who-knows-what with it behind the counter. If they try to use your card to pay for a meal for one of their friends, it's easier to discover the error. The best advice, though, is to pay cash for your meals, thus eliminating the risk altogether, especially if you are visiting a restaurant you have never visited before.

Another area to watch carefully is your physical mailbox. If you live in a rough area or even near one, you may want to consider opening up a post office box and having your mail delivered to a secure location where you can pick it up yourself. Thieves can snatch up your mail while you are at work, and they will be happy to thumb through your junk mail looking for nuggets of information they may use against you. I'm a jogger, and on one afternoon, I found a whole armful of opened mail addressed to a nearby business on the side of the road. I wondered what the thief had been looking for. My guess was that he was trying to find checks written to the company. He probably wouldn't risk trying to cash the check himself, but now he has the customers' bank account numbers and addresses they sent to that company. He can easily order checks online with his own name printed on them, and before the customers know it, they will see checks they did not write flowing through their accounts. The moral of this story is that if you send a check to a company for payment, verify by balancing your checkbook that the company actually received the check and cashed it, removing money from your account. If it's been several weeks and the check still hasn't been cashed, you should call them and ask if they have it and why they aren't cashing it. If they say they never received your check, call your bank and ask for advice on how you can be protected. You may want to change bank account numbers just to be on the safe side.

Some people say that online banking is too dangerous and they are content to continue writing checks. There are risks when you bank online, but you need to be aware that you are taking equally dangerous risks when you put that check in the mail. In all my years of online banking, I have not experienced any problems. Of course, I also go through the extra precautions of using a computer that only I have access to and that I don't use for surfing, gaming, and what-not. However, I have run across issue when mailing checks, such as the time my mail was delivered to the wrong address. A check written to me was delivered two houses down from where I live. The recipients opened my letter without realizing that it was not addressed to them. They could easily have used the information on that check to their advantage or possibly even tried to cash the check themselves. Fortunately for me, they brought me the check and apologized for opening the letter. In another letter I received from my company, my birthdate was actually written in the letter. Your birthdate and social security number are examples of common security codes that many companies will use to verify who you are. If your company is writing the full values for these security codes on letters they are sending you, kindly inform them of the potential security risks and ask them to only use a portion of the code, such as the last four digits. If such a letter is accidentally sent to the wrong address, someone may now have a piece of information he might need to gain access to your financial assets.

Identity theft is a growing problem, so you must do what you can to protect your family's finances. One of the best ways to do this is by balancing your checkbook each month. In this day and age, I would even go so far as to recommend a weekly or daily check on the activity in your bank account or credit card to make sure you don't see anything suspicious. If an illicit transaction is detected and reported quickly enough, the bank will most likely cover some or all of your losses.

REASON 3 – YOU ARE FLAWED

I hate to burst your bubble, but yes, you are flawed, just like me, which is why you need to balance your checkbook on a monthly basis to check for your own mistakes. Because I'm human, just as you are, I make plenty of mistakes. I've balanced my checkbook for years, but even so, several times throughout the year, I will write down the wrong amount or forget to write something down altogether. These are easy mistakes to make, especially as you use your debit card more frequently and the number of transactions hitting your account increases. Also, if you have a spouse who uses the same account, he or she may forget to tell you about a purchase. Usually, one person in the family will be responsible for keeping up with the checkbook. If you are not that person, keep all your receipts and pass them along to your spouse each day so he or she can record what was spent. It's best to do this on a daily basis while the transaction is still fresh in your mind. When you work on your budget, you will be classifying these expenses in a few different categories. It's helpful to know what the money was spent for and whether that expense was something previously budgeted or something that wasn't budgeted before. For example, if later in the week you see an entry in the checkbook for the grocery store, you might ask yourself, "Was this for the budgeted groceries, a pick-up item, or a prescription?" You may never know unless you write down a little note that tells you what it was for, rather than simply writing "grocery store" or relying upon a vague memory.

Most of the mistakes I make are in the amount I write in the checkbook. I may have misread the amount on the receipt, forgot to include the tip, or neglected to write the thing down at all. Sometimes I'll get a receipt from the merchant that is only a blank piece of paper because they haven't put fresh ink in the machine in weeks. I especially love it when the receipt printer at the gas station is out of ink or paper. If this happens to you, while the amount is still fresh on your mind, ask the clerk for a receipt you can read or write down the amount right then and there. If you wait, you'll forget how much you spent, and you'll have to trust that the bank recorded the right amount. Sometimes I think merchants use that magical disappearing ink when printing receipts. I keep all my receipts in case I need to return something, and I've noticed more and more that the ink fades after a few months, making them almost unreadable. I have old school papers written several years ago by my kids, and the ink seems as fresh as they day they turned in the paper. Perhaps the merchant doesn't want you to return anything. If you don't have a receipt that can be read, you might be denied credit. You may want to go so far as to make a copy of the receipt, to scan it into your computer as an image, or to snap a picture of it with your smart phone. In any case, when you go through the process of balancing your checkbook, you'll easily find and correct clerical errors resulting from these hard-to-read receipts.

Another common mistake is to expect that when you pay for something with your debit card and then return the product for a refund, the money is placed back into your account as quickly as it was taken out. However, the money is never returned that quickly, especially if the store processes your return as a credit card transaction instead of a debit transaction. They control when to send the return amount to the banks for processing, and some merchants can take thirty days or more to send in returns. They like to keep hold of the money as long as possible! Sure, you'll get a receipt right away, and if you are like me, you'll mark it down in your checkbook as money back in the bank. Don't count your chickens until they hatch, though. Verify the return has actually been deposited into your account before writing it down in your checkbook. You risk bouncing a check if you think you have more money than you really do. If the return is for a large amount, ask instead for cash or for a check you can cash right away. I returned an item for several thousand dollars once, and although I had a nice receipt in my hand, it took the merchant nearly three weeks to send the money to the banks. Learn from my mistakes! Ask for cash or check! Another time, I took my vehicle in for repairs, and the shop accidentally debited my card twice for the same amount. I quickly caught their error and called them the next day. To my surprise, they admitted the mistake, but told me the extra $450 they took out of my checking account may take a couple of weeks to clear the banks. It sure didn't take a couple of weeks for them to take the money out of my account, so why should I have to suffer for their mistake? I insisted on receiving a check right then and there, and they finally saw that it was the right thing to do. Mistakes like that can really take a toll on someone just trying to make ends meet, especially if they do not use a credit card or do not have significant reserves to fall back on. Don't be afraid to push back on merchants and insist they do the right thing.

REASON 4 – EMERGING TECHNOLOGIES

If you start using some of these fancy new technological methods to pay for your goods, you need to balance your checkbook on a monthly basis. I told you earlier that the use of cash will soon be extinct, but did you know that credit cards and bank cards (the thin plastic things in your wallet) won't be too far behind on the extinction list? These things are easily lost or bent, and when you have a lot of them, they are a pain to carry around. Banks and credit card companies are working on new ways to pay using a technology called Near Field Communication (NFC). Special computer radio-frequency identification (RFID) chips are embedded in a credit card, key ring, or similar device. Retailers have special point of sale devices that can read your financial account information directly from these chips. To pay for your transaction, all you have to do is wave your RFID enabled credit cards or device near the reader and it detects that you want to pay using that service. The account information is read from the RFID chip and the transaction is complete. Companies advertise that using these special cards or devices is less risky than the traditional method of handing the card over to the clerk or swiping your card and entering your personal identification number (PIN). The clerk can make note of the security code on the back of your card, and the next person in line can watch you enter your PIN, both of which are security risks. With the wave device, you keep your card in hand, and you do not have to physically enter a security code or PIN, supposedly reducing the risk of fraud. This technology requires a phone or credit card that can transmit and receive financial data, but wave devices, or "mobile wallets," as they are also known, are becoming more common every day.

As with any emerging technology, of course, there are still going to be risks, and you need to be looking out for fraud or errors. I was shopping recently and noticed a variety of new steel wallets. At the time, I wondered to myself why anyone would ever want a metal wallet or purse. Later, though, I saw on the news that organized crime was beginning to take advantage of those individuals who carry a wave device. The criminals had a large bag in hand that contained a special reader. As the criminals walked by someone with a wave device, they would capture the financial information from the unsuspecting individual and use the stolen information to gain access to their assets. If you have an RFID-enabled credit card or device, take the extra precaution to get a wallet or purse that prevents others from reading your account information.

Another way to enable your phone as a mobile wallet is to download a mobile wallet app that allows you to link your bank or credit card to the app and to the video camera on your phone. When you make your purchase, the retailer displays a QR code (those funny-looking square bar codes) for you to scan with your camera. You open your mobile wallet app, scan the code, and like magic, your purchase is complete! These systems are starting to find more widespread use, so if you try them out, look out for errors by making sure you balance your checkbook.

As a side note, those QR codes contain much more than the simple set of numbers you would find on a traditional bar code. Scanning one can take you directly to a particular website, start the installation of an app, and more. If you have a smart phone, scan the safe QR code here for a secret message! However, don't go around randomly scanning everything you see just to satisfy your curiosity. Beware of scam QR codes used to introduce a virus into your device or trick you into releasing details about yourself and your identity.

A time may soon come when everyone may be required to carry a national ID card. These will be promoted as a way for governments to cut costs, crack down on corruption, and ensure everyone is paying their fair share in taxes. Without this card, you will not be able to open a bank account or even obtain a job. Because standard ID cards with the magnetic strip on the back are made of the same flawed plastic that can be bent, burnt, lost, or demagnetized, and because they carry a limited amount of information about the card holder, they will likely be replaced with RFID-enabled cards or similar devices. These little boogers can be as small as the tip of a pencil, yet they carry comprehensive personal details such as your health vitals (allergies, blood type, etc.), your financial information, and more.

Today, RFID-enabled IDs are used in the pet industry to help owners locate their lost animals. The pet has the RFID device loaded with the owner's information implanted under its skin. Many veterinarians have RFID readers that they use to identify lost pets. India, which boasts one of world's largest populations at over 1 billion people, started implementation of their RFID-enabled national ID cards back in September of 2010. Corruption in the social services area in India is rampant. I have a friend from India with whom I work, and he says America is an honest place to live. In the United States, for the most part, the system works and people pay their bills. This is not the case in India, he tells me. The ID system means to eliminate all fraud by requiring all citizens of India to carry RFID cards that collect biometrics such as fingerprints and iris scans. Many do not realize it, but our former president George W. Bush signed into law a similar national ID system called the Real ID Act, enacted May 11, 2005. As I write this book, implementation of the Real ID Act has been delayed, but unless further delays are specifically requested and granted, it is scheduled to be implemented in the near future. Just something to keep an eye on as these emerging technologies begin to take hold.

REASON 5 –SAVE MONEY

If you balance your checkbook on a monthly basis, you can save yourself some serious money. Many wonder why they can't just go online to make sure they have the money in the bank to cover their purchase. Sometimes, however, it can take days or even weeks for certain transactions to clear your bank account, especially if you are using an online bill paying service. How can you ever know exactly how much you can safely spend if you never know how much you have left in your checkbook? "I have overdraft protection," you proudly boast. What you are really saying is, "I am too lazy to spend ten minutes a month to keep my checkbook balanced, and I will gladly pay the bank a hefty penalty and interest on any checks that bounce or go into overdraft protection. If the bank makes a mistake, it doesn't bother me because I won't know about it." What's worse, there are laws against writing bad checks, so you are risking your reputation and livelihood. You don't want your name listed next to the cash register along with a note that says in big, bold, black letters, "Do not accept checks from Mr. Unbalanced." You don't need that in your life right now. Spend the ten minutes and get your checkbook balanced. For just ten short minutes, you get peace of mind, knowledge of how much you can safely spend, and more money in your pocket since no more checks are bouncing and no more payments of interest are going towards overdraft protection services.

REASON 6 – TO MAKE YOUR BUDGET WORK

The last reason to balance your checkbook on a monthly basis (although I'm sure there are more) is to obtain an accurate picture of how much money you have to work with when starting your budget. When considering how much you can spend during a given month, you don't just look at your monthly income; you also look at how much you already have in your bank account. Sure, it may be only a few dollars, but it is real money that is already available. One of biggest problems many have to deal with is cash flow. You might make enough money to pay your bills, but unfortunately, some of those bills come due before you get paid, and you end up having to pay them late with added interest and fees. You will need to learn how to build up an emergency fund so you will always have some money to work with at the start of each month. Not only can an emergency fund be used to help relieve the stress of cash flow problems, it is a tremendous comfort in itself.

YOU DON'T HAVE TO BE AN ACCOUNTANT

I am amazed by the number of people who refuse to keep their checkbooks balanced. You would think, at least for the six reasons I listed above, that everyone would do it. Some, however, think this is the job of an accountant, and since they can't afford a personal accountant, the checkbook never gets balanced.

If you don't know how to balance your checkbook, ask your bank or a friend who has done it before. Also, there are usually instructions on the back of your banking statement describing all the steps required for the process. Don't let some computer software try to do it for you; you will remain in the dark forever! See Figure 3-1 for my easy instructions on how you can balance your own checkbook.

For those of you who have never balanced your checkbook before, you may find it difficult the first time. You might have made a mistake several months (or even years) ago, and the chances of finding that mistake are slim to none. But that's okay. You should make an effort to make sure all the checks you have written have at least been cashed. Beyond that, to keep it simple, figure out the difference between what you calculated from Figure 3-1 and what the bank says you have, and then make an entry in your checkbook for that exact difference. You might put in the description something like "first checkbook balancing." Don't forget to put a checkmark next to this item. Repeat the instructions found in Figure 3-1 and now you should see that your checkbook is balanced! There's a chance you might have to make an adjusting entry like this in the next month or so, but once you become more diligent in keeping your checkbook up to date, you shouldn't have as many problems, at least in my experience.

If you still don't balance after several attempts, don't get frustrated, especially if this is your first attempt at balancing your checkbook. You may have never even used a checkbook register before, so you may not have anything to balance your bank statement against. If you don't have a checkbook register, ask the bank for one. They will usually give you one for free, especially if you have an account with them. Without a prior record of balancing, you must trust that what the bank reports is accurate. Start by writing down what the bank says is your starting balance. Then record all transactions the bank says they have processed, adding or subtracting from your starting balance as needed. Your ending balance should match theirs. Now think hard and write down any transactions that have occurred since the bank statement was sent. You might need to go online to your bank's website and see if you missed anything. There is still a chance you might miss something, like a check that hasn't been cashed yet. You'll discover those next time, but in the meantime, pay close attention to your balance in case you have missed a large amount.

5 Simple Steps to Balancing Your Checkbook

You'll need:
1. Your last bank statement
2. Your checkbook
3. A calculator

Steps :
1. Look over the bank statement. Verify that you have written down in your checkbook each deposit, check, debit card use, and any other miscellaneous fees shown on the bank statement. I like to put checkmarks next to each item in both the statement and my checkbook. That way, I know I have it covered. By checking items off as I go, I have found many times when I wrote something down twice in my checkbook, wrote the wrong amount, or forgot to write it down (an easy mistake to make when your spouse also has access to the account). After comparing your bank statement and checkbook, you will most likely have a few deposits, checks, or online transactions that do not have a checkmark next to them. That's fine; it just means the bank hasn't recorded it yet. It could also mean that the person you paid hasn't cashed the check yet. I have found sometimes when using online bill pay, the date the payment is processed is sometimes a week or so later.
2. Write down what the bank says your ending balance was at the time they printed your bank statement.
3. Add up all the deposits in your checkbook that do not have a checkmark next to them (the bank doesn't know about these yet).
4. Add up all the expenses in your checkbook that do not have a checkmark next to them (the bank doesn't know about these yet either).
5. Apply this simple formula using your calculator to see if it matches the ending balance in your checkbook:

	Bank Statement Ending Balance (from 2 above)
plus	Deposits the bank hasn't recorded yet (from 3 above)
minus	Expenses the bank hasn't recorded yet (from 4 above)
equals	Your checkbook balance!

If the two balances don't match, go back and check that the amounts you wrote down match what the bank has. I have also made the mistake of not adding or subtracting correctly. Go back and check your math! Once you do this a few times, you'll find you can easily balance your checkbook each month in five to ten minutes!

FIGURE 3-1

INTRODUCING ONLINE CALCULATORS

On our website budgetsteward.com, we also provide a number of online calculators to help you with specific financial questions, as shown on Figure 3-2.

Budgeting
- Account Reconciliation
- Recommended Percents
- Irregular Payments
- Net Worth

Dealing with Debt
- Accelerated Debt Payoff
- Debt Consolidation
- Debt Payoff Goal
- Debt Ratio

Credit Cards
- Credit Card Comparision
- Minimum Payment Interest
- Principle / Interest
- Fixed vs Minimum

Loans Part 1
- Bi-Weekly vs Monthly
- Loan Comparison
- Loan Amortization
- Missing Loan Term

Loans Part 2
- Simple Loan
- Mortgage Payoff Goal
- Mortgage Refinance
- Rent vs Buy

FIGURE 3-2

You can simplify your checkbook balancing process by clicking on the Account Reconciliation calculator in the Budgeting section of the online calculators, as shown on Figure 3-3.

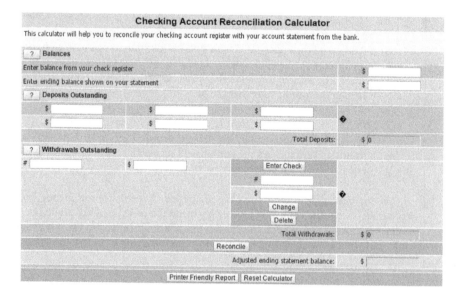

FIGURE 3-3

You use the same process as described in Figure 3-2. The online calculator just makes it easy for you. After entering the required information and pressing the Reconcile button, you are shown whether you are balanced or whether you are off and by how much. Most calculators, like this one, have a printer friendly report so you can print the results for your records.

KEEPING IT SIMPLE

Since we are on the subject of checkbooks, how many accounts do you have? If the answer is more than one, you may have more than one too many! Our goal is simplification. When someone can prove to me that it is simpler to balance two checking statements than to balance one, I'll gladly open another account. For husbands and wives, do you each have your own account? Is this your attitude: what's hers is hers and what's his is his? Do you each have your own bills? Are you saying, "I don't trust him (or her) with my money and I want to make sure I still have money left over in my account so I can buy the things I want"? It sure does seem as though there are a lot of "I"s in that statement. If you want to continue to live this way, you might need two budgets, one for each account. This is fine, and some people are more comfortable operating that way. Separate accounts offer a level of control to each person, and it may be difficult to relinquish that control. They do make planning things together a little more challenging, because it may not be evident how much extra money you have to do some of the things you want to do. Combining checking accounts should at least be a consideration, though.

A BALANCED BUDGET

It's amazing to see what a difficult time our government has trying to get a proposed budget passed into law. Even if they are lucky enough to get a budget passed, chances are it's not going to be balanced. In all likelihood, they are going to be running the country with a deficit, spending more money than they have coming in through tax revenues. Each year, that deficit adds to our national debt, which is basically a huge loan that our government owes to various entities and has to pay interest on. That's where the danger comes in. When the amount of interest you have to pay on your debt becomes so large you can't even pay your other bills, something has got to give. Usually, that means the taxpayers have to give more taxes. Perhaps some of the government agencies have to give more by reducing programs or benefits. It could mean that the government simply prints more money, which increases our national debt even more. Unfortunately, you don't have a money printing machine or an endless supply of money. You might have to make quick decisions to make sure you have enough money to pay remaining bills when they come due. That's where a balanced budget can help.

A balanced checkbook is your first step to being able to prepare a balanced budget, but there is a major difference between the two. A balanced checkbook simply means that you and the bank agree on how much money you currently have in the bank. A balanced budget means that your expected income for the month (which includes what you already have in your account) equals expected expenses. The task of balancing your budget can be a little challenging at first, but we'll show you how to do it, going over the steps to make sure it works and the reasons why it needs to be done. After you set your initial budget and start depositing money and paying bills, your budget becomes a reflection of the current state of your finances, taking into consideration the money you have already deposited and still have to deposit, as well as the bills you have already paid and have still yet to pay. It's easy (and expected) for your budget to become unbalanced as you go through the month. Your budget is the tool you use to decide whether additional actions are required to get it back in balance.

If you want to have a balanced budget, does that mean you have to spend every dime you make? The answer is no. You don't necessarily have to spend every dime, but you need to decide what to do with every dime – whether it is setting it aside in savings, or for a future non-monthly expense, or to go towards your next financial goal. This process is called naming every dollar. You are telling each dollar you earn what you want to do with it. Let's say for example, you go through the budgeting process at the start of the month and you see where you have more income than expenses. That's great, but what do you decide to do with the extra income? If you decide nothing, the likelihood that extra income will be spent on something unimportant or frivolous increases exponentially. That's why it is so important at the beginning of the month to decide what's important, what goals you want to work to achieve, and how every dollar should be spent. Then, when frivolous opportunities arise, you can easily see the impact that will have in making progress toward your goals. So, is it more important to go out on the town, or do we need to save the money for an upcoming vacation? Balancing your budget helps keep everything in perspective, helping you realize what's important and what's not.

WHEN IS IT OK <u>NOT</u> TO BALANCE YOUR CHECKBOOK?

Ok, reality check. There are a few situations where balancing your checkbook is not really all that necessary. For example, let's look at the life of a teenager or college student. Most do not have any bills to pay for, and whatever money they earn through part-time or summer work is mostly disposable income. They will cash their check, and spend it on things like gas, eating out with friends, movies, clothes, etc. Banks are good about showing the updated balance almost immediately. Cash flow is not an issue for these because most do not have any upcoming bills to pay for. To keep life "simple", encourage them to pay close attention to the balance in their account, and also to the transactions that take money from their account.

The other class of individuals that may see limited benefit from balancing their checkbook are those that have chosen, or now have, a simplified lifestyle, where the number of bank transactions is minimal. Of course, for such a person, balancing their checkbook would be really easy!

For most of us though, the number of transactions will be such that we really need to balance our checkbook regularly just to make sure we didn't miss anything, and to make sure we have enough money in our checking account to pay the bills when they come due. Even for the teen or college student, now is the time to start teaching them how to balance their checkbook so that when they do get out on their own, they won't dig themselves into a mess that will be extremely painful to get out of.

WEEK 3 – QUESTIONS & DISCUSSION
(You may copy this page as needed)

1. What does it mean when your checkbook is balanced?

   _____

   _____

   _____

2. How does balancing your checkbook save you money?

   _____

   _____

   _____

3. TRUE or FALSE.
   When you return an item to the store for a refund and ask them to put it back on your card, the money is immediately deposited into your account as required by law.

4. What is happening when you are being spoofed?

   _____

   _____

   _____

5. Name three reasons why you should balance your checkbook each month.

   _____

   _____

   _____

6. For those that don't balance their checkbook, what is a typical reason why?

   _____

   _____

7. PRACTICE.
   Balance your checkbook using the "5 Simple Steps".

WEEK 4 - MY GOALS

The next important step to successful budgeting is to define the reasons why you want a budget in the first place. These are your goals. Why is this important to you? The reasons you list will become your motivation not to give up on your budgeting program. Let's face it, who wants to take the time to sit at a table and put all this stuff together? It's not a lot of fun. It seems as though you have hundreds of better and more important things to do.

DISTRACTIONS

It is really easy these days to come up with an excuse for not doing something. Most of us are exhausted by the time we get home from work, and all we want to do is eat our supper and take a few moments to veg in front of the TV. I have to confess that I can be one of the world's worst procrastinators. Even after my wife writes me an official "honey-do" list, I have found that it may take months before I am able to get a particular chore finished. Why is that? Is it because I am lazy? Am I really that tired? It's a hard question to answer, but first you must answer the question, "What could I or should I be doing at this very moment?" An honest answer to this question will reveal where you are placing your priorities and where your focus is. The answer might very well be that you should be sitting down and resting from your work, relaxing your mind. Your mind and body do need rest, but how much is enough? Is bedtime close enough that you could be doing something more productive now and resting later when you go to bed? Only you can answer these types of questions. I try to go out jogging during my lunch hour at least two to three times a week. I could be doing many other things with that time, but instead, I choose to jog because my health is a priority. It isn't much fun, but after I finish my run, I feel refreshed and I'm glad that I did it. Where are your priorities?

It's time to get off the couch and think about the really important things in your life. Think about it: the average lifespan is somewhere in the seventies. If you live to age seventy-five, that's only 27,375 days in your life to make something of yourself. After you take away the time growing up, sleeping, and making a living, what are your left with? The clock is ticking and time is wasting. There is no time like the present to work toward fulfilling your dreams. It doesn't matter what your age is; you can start anytime.

Setting goals is not a task you should take lightly. Careful planning is required. Unless you plan ahead, you could end up going the wrong direction.

How will you ever be able to achieve any goal unless you start planning today? As the old saying goes, people don't plan to fail, they fail to plan. You need to predetermine the proper course of action that leads you to the finish line. Setting goals will require you to adjust your priorities. Instead of doing the same things day after day and month after month, you will have to make some lifestyle changes, and some of these changes may be pretty dramatic. If you are married and have a family, you definitely need to talk to them about your goals and the changes that might be required. Don't expect a warm welcome all the time, though. In fact, you might get so much resistance that you may need to reconsider your goals, or at least the timing of your goals. They may have their own goals that they want considered. Now is the time to communicate, communicate, and communicate. In fact, you might suggest a goal and then allow some time for that thought to sink in with other family members. At first, they may think you have fallen off your rocker, but give it time. Be prepared to explain the benefits of working toward achieving that goal. Then give it some more time.

Once everyone is on board, it's time for action. You will need to break down your goal into as many workable chunks as you can. Don't believe that this is going to be a cakewalk. You will encounter problems as you work to complete your goal. Large goals are especially hard because sometimes it appears that very little progress is being made and the end is nowhere in sight. Every month, something will always come up to try to derail you, distract you, and discourage you from moving forward. By expecting the unexpected, you can make allowances for many of these issues and still be able to make progress on a regular basis. Make sure you review how you are progressing and report milestones to your family to keep them engaged and excited as you move forward. You may even want to build some breaks into your goals to celebrate how far you have made it. These breaks will provide much-needed breathers, not only to you but also to your family.

GOAL COMBINATIONS

There are many different types of goals, from short-term to long-term. Most of you probably have your mind set on some financial goals right now, some which could be short-term, like paying off a bill, while others are long-term, like getting completely out of debt. Did you know that your goals can also be inward-facing or outward-facing? An inward-facing goal is one for which you are the primary beneficiary once the goal is accomplished. An example of this might be saving enough money for a new motorcycle. I've always wanted one just because they look like so much fun to ride, and I would try to justify it by saying how much money I will save in gas. But deep down, I know I am going to be the primary beneficiary once that goal is achieved. That's not necessarily a bad thing, but it is something to keep in mind as you work on all your goals, making sure you have the right balance. On the other side of the ledger, you have outward-facing goals. An example of this might be saving enough money to pay for a skating party for my kids and their friends. Although I do still love to skate, I know my family and friends would love this much more, and thus I am not the primary beneficiary. That's also something that shouldn't take much effort to accomplish and could be done in a relatively short time period. You won't get much flak from family members, as this is something they can all enjoy. You are looking out for others. You are a good citizen, a good parent, and a good friend. As you can see, your reward for completing outward-facing goals is sometimes very different from inward-facing goals.

Let's take a minute and review the types of goals we have so far. I think you'll be surprised at the number of combinations.

1. Short-term vs. long-term
2. Inward-facing vs. outward-facing
3. Financial vs. non-financial

Based on the above, you can have eight different combinations of goals, like a short-term, inward-facing, financial goal. You can easily determine which combination is going to be more difficult to achieve. Long-term is more difficult than short-term simply because of the long time it takes to accomplish and the high chances of giving up or being forced to quit. Inward-facing is more difficult than outward-facing because others may not share your enthusiasm, as the goal has little or no value to them, only to you. Why should they go the extra mile to accommodate you on a goal like that? Financial goals are more difficult than non-financial goals because money is hard to come by. I'm still waiting on that tree in my back yard to sprout dollar bills instead of leaves.

Putting all these together, you can see that a long-term, inward-facing, financial goal is going to be the most difficult and most challenging type of goal to achieve. You'll get resistance not only at the beginning but also along the way as you work your goal, and you may get more resistance and possibly even resentment after you achieve it. Some may even call you selfish. Be careful when adding these goals to your list. There will be plenty of landmines to avoid. Goals of this kind are not easily accomplished in one month. They are likely to take away some of the funds you have set aside for entertainment and dining out. You can easily see where friction is going to occur. People normally do not like change. Most like to live in a stable environment because of the security that lifestyle brings them. Start taking things away in order to achieve a goal like this, and you're likely to stir up some heated discussion.

On the opposite side, it is easy to see that a short-term, outward-facing, non-financial goal will be the easiest type of goal to achieve. Short-term is easy because it is something achieved now or in the very near future. You can taste it! Outward-facing is easy because others get to participate and to enjoy the fruits of your labor. Non-financial is easy because it's free! Put as many of these as time allows on your list; you can't go wrong here.

What does non-financial mean? Is it anything other than money? It could be, but I would like you to begin thinking about goals that bring you closer to achieving your purpose in this life, as we talked about at the end of Week One. The concept may sound strange, but as I mentioned earlier, a purpose-driven individual is much more inclined to move heaven and earth in order to fulfill their purpose. Why? A purpose-driven individual is happy in doing what they are doing. It's like falling in love for the first time. You'll do anything to nurture the relationship, going the extra mile to impress and making sure you do all you can to keep it going. It's a great feeling, and fulfilling a purpose-driven goal can feel just as good. Most likely, that goal will be outward-facing, and it may seem to be a non-financial goal until you take the time to break it down into all the steps needed to accomplish it. Some parts of a purpose-driven goal are probably going to require money while others will not; therefore, we'll put it in between a financial goal and a non-financial goal. Our goal combinations now look like this:

1. Short-term vs. long-term
2. Inward-facing vs. outward-facing
3. Financial vs. purpose-driven vs. non-financial

Now we are up to 12 different possible combinations!

YOUR BUCKET LIST

Next, we'll practice putting together some goals. Some people like to have fun with their goals and dreams and create what they call their "bucket list." These are the things the person hopes to accomplish before they "kick the bucket," or die. Goals most people like to include on their list include jumping from an airplane (hopefully with a parachute, or else they'll be kicking the bucket a lot sooner), travelling to some exotic foreign location, and getting married. As for my list, I would like to ride on a gondola through the canals of Venice, visit Jerusalem, and sail to a deserted island and explore it. Just for fun, list your top ten bucket list items in Figure 4-1.

Bucket Item	Description
1	
2	
3	
4	
5	
6	
7	
8	
9	
10	

FIGURE 4-1

How did you do on yours? Not so easy, is it? Were you able to come up with ten? Let's take a look at what you've written down. Beside each goal, classify each one using the different combinations of possible goals we discussed earlier. Do you have both inward-facing and outward-facing goals? Are some of your goals short-term while others are long-term? Will some require a tremendous amount of cash while others do not? Would you classify any of these as a purpose-driven goal? Now you can start to see which ones are more important, which ones are just for fun, and which ones you'll likely to get acceptance for from the rest of the family.

It's harder than most people think to create a bucket list. On one hand, you don't want to limit yourself, but on the other hand, you feel that some of your goals are totally unrealistic and could never be achieved. You don't trust in your abilities because your goal is something you have never done or experienced. I was a really picker eater when I was growing up. Even in my young adult life, I never ate salads, Chinese, Mexican, or Italian food. I was afraid I wouldn't like them because of the look and smell. I had never experienced those foods before, and my taste buds were basically set on frozen dinners and canned spaghetti. As soon as I was married, however, my wife dragged me to a Mexican restaurant. I tried some of the food, but still wasn't too sure I liked it. She loved it, though, so she dragged me back for more. After several years of these sorts of excursions, I now love Mexican, Chinese, Italian, and yes, even salads! Don't limit your goals simply because it is something you have never experienced. Try it, you'll like it; or at least, so the old commercial says.

Now let's take a closer look at your bucket list. Not every one of your goals will require money in order to achieve it. Find the ones that you know will take money, and pick the one you would like to do first. I know many of you are thinking to yourself there is no way you can accomplish that goal, especially in the bad financial shape you are in. Just keep in mind, there is a 100% failure rate for those who never try. You can do this. Whenever I want or need something from someone, I always ask for it, but many people don't even try. They are afraid the answer will be "No." If you never ask, though, the answer always will be "No." There's nothing to be lost by asking. Stop telling yourself you can't do it, and don't be afraid to try something new.

Begin to think about everything that's required to mark your chosen item off your list. Let's take my trip to Venice, for example. I'm going to need a passport, a plane ticket, a place to stay, money for the gondola, and more. I can see it's not going to be an easy task to accomplish, but anything worthwhile is going to take some effort. Let's start off small, then. My first goal is to get my passport. I will need to find out how much a passport costs, where to go to get one, and what kind of documentation they require. Then I must secure the documentation and take the time to go apply. With all these steps, something as simple as getting a passport can easily become overwhelming to many people. However, once I figure out the cost, I can put that amount of money, or a portion of it, into my budget as a goal to save for. I may not have a lot of extra money to spend on extra items, but what if I only took ten dollars a month and stuffed it away in an envelope? How long would it take me to save enough money to pay for the passport then? Whatever your first bucket list goal may be, simply note the total cost of the first item you need to get closer to marking it off. We'll determine later how much you can safely set aside for it and how long it will take before you can go get it.

PURPOSE-DRIVEN GOALS

Now let's take it to the next level and see if we can define some of your purpose-driven goals. Why were you put on this earth in the first place? Take some time to think about it. Talk with friends and family, ask them what their purpose is, and then ask them what they think your purpose is. What do you consider to be priorities in your life? Some people might list their priorities in the following order:

1. Faith
2. Family
3. Job
4. Community
5. Self

Many would say most of their purpose-driven goals are based on one of these priorities. In some parts of the world, adherence to the doctrines of the dominant faith is the sole purpose in individuals' lives. Other people are driven to raise their family, grow their career, and contribute to their community. It's all based on the gifts and talents you have been given and what you choose to do with them. Your primary purpose may span more than one of these priorities, as it's hard for them not to overlap. You may need to work on one in order to achieve the other. For example, you might need to work on yourself, giving yourself a better education, in order to get a better job and build a career so that you can take care of your family and do the things you believe you are called to do. Each goal can build on the other. Just because you are doing something for yourself does not necessarily make it an inward-facing goal, either. You may be working to improve yourself to make life better not only for you but also for those around you, so don't feel bad if you have to invest a little in yourself. One of my purpose-driven goals is to teach folks how to put together a budget that fits their lifestyle. That's why I teach budgeting classes, why I wrote this book, and why I developed budgeting software based on the concepts taught in this book. You can see how my purpose-driven goal spans multiple priorities. Take a few minutes now and list some of your purpose-driven goals in Figure 4-2.

Priority	Purpose-Driven Goal
1	
2	
3	
4	
5	
6	
7	
8	
9	
10	

FIGURE 4-2

Just like the bucket list, it may not be easy for you to list your purpose-driven goals at this time. If so, start at the bottom. How can you improve yourself? What will you then do with the new and improved you?

Since this is a budgeting book, I am ultimately trying to get you to define those goals that require money. After all, for most people, the main reason they are not making progress towards their goals is because of their lack of money. Hopefully, you now have a rough draft of your bucket list and your purpose driven goals, although you may not have a clue how to go about fulfilling them. We will use this information to help us complete our list of financial goals. Once we have our financial goals defined, we can move forward with the budgeting process so we can begin to make progress and accomplish those goals.

FINANCIALLY-DRIVEN GOALS

Financially-driven goals are much easier to define than purpose-driven goals. Examples include paying off a bill you are making monthly payments on, building up a reserve of money to provide security and a cushion in case something bad or unexpected happens, or achieving goals on your bucket list or your purpose-driven goals that you know require finances in order to be completed. That's a lot of goals to consider, and it can seem overwhelming. I can tell you now that most of you are not going to be able to include all your financial goals in your first budget. Which ones are more important? If you paid off some debt, that would leave you more money to focus on other goals. But what if you are so much in debt that if you were to focus only on paying it off, you would never have any money for your other goals? It's hard to say what the right course of action is because each person's circumstances are unique. However, I have some of my own financial goals I want to suggest to you to get you started, and then I'll give you some guidance on when to start mixing in your other financial goals.

FINANCIAL GOAL #1 – YOUR CASH STASH

The first financial goal you'll work on is your cash stash. A cash stash is money you have stored in a safe place in your home. It is preferable, though, that you not put the money in a jar and bury it in your backyard, only to be found decades later by treasure hunters. Your cash stash is important for a number of reasons. If there is a major power outage, stores may remain open, but only for those who can pay with cash. Your cash stash is also the beginning of your reserves, to be tapped when something unexpected happens, such as when family members and friends run into an emergency. Wouldn't it be good to have access to a little cash to help out a friend in need? It's always good to have a little cash on hand. We're not talking about a lot of money here; I recommend about a $250 cash stash. It may take you a few months to accumulate this much, but it should take priority over all your other goals. I have found through personal experience that it can be hard to maintain even a cash stash as small as $50, but don't give up. Keep building it up until you have achieved your goal. Make sure you keep it in a safe place and don't advertise the location or the amount of money you have in your stash to anyone other than your spouse. You don't want to paint a target on yourself, advertising to the world how much cash you have in the house. If you do use some of your cash stash, replenishing it should become your top priority again.

FINANCIAL GOAL #2 – YOUR "GRAND" RESERVES

Once your cash stash is set, your next priority is to build a $1,000 (a grand) reserve of money in your checking account. We'll work on building this up much more later on, but for now, we need to get it up to $1,000. Why $1,000? I have found that most common household and car repairs, such as an air conditioner, a refrigerator, a leaking water pipe, a washer or dryer, or any number of other household appliances, will normally set you back several hundred dollars. Having the $1,000 in reserve will give you the comfort and security your family needs, letting them know that if something unexpected does happen, you have a reserve on hand for just such an emergency. Believe me, things are going to break down through normal wear and tear. Without this reserve, you may be forced to make some very unpopular decisions on what to do without for the month so you can pay for the repair. Worse, you may be forced to pay for the repair on credit, in which case you will be charged interest. It's better to be prepared, just as the Boy Scouts motto says you should be. If you do need to use some or all of your reserve, replenishing it should become priority again.

There are not many people who can easily throw $1,000 into their reserves in one month, so you'll need to build it up. Once you go through the entire budgeting process in *Week 7 - My First Budget*, you'll know how much you can safely apply each month.

FINANCIAL GOAL #3 – LARGE RECURRING HEADACHES

You've got your cash stash and a cool grand in reserves in your checking account. Next, we need to take inventory of those pesky bills that come due once a quarter, every 6 months, or every year. These are bills such as car insurance, car taxes, house insurance, house taxes, vacations, and holidays. These bills are usually for a large sum of money, and they can wreak havoc on a family during the month they come due. It's extremely difficult to come up with such large sums of cash all at once. Instead of waiting until the month the bill comes due, however, why not set aside a little money each month so that when this large bill comes due, the money will already be in the bank, and you'll be ready to pay for it. I have found many families that are forced to do without necessities of life such as food or gas because every bit of money that comes in has to be put toward the large bill. Even worse, many will not pay on time, and thus they risk lapsing their insurance policy and receiving bad marks on their credit report.

To work non-monthly bills into your budget, all you need to do is divide the total bill payment by the number of months before the bill is due. The result will be the amount of money you set aside each month. For example, let's suppose you pay your car insurance every six months, and it costs you $300. If you only have four months to come up with the money, how much money would you need to save during each of those four months? All you need to do is divide $300 by 4, which is $75. That's the amount of money you need to set aside each month. At the end of the month, either stuff this money in an envelope or leave it in your checking account and let it accumulate. If you leave it in your checking account, you need to realize when the month is over that the money left is set aside for a future expense and is not to be spent. Those just starting out on a budget may not have the discipline to do this, so I would recommend taking that money out of your checking account and sticking it in an envelope, building it up there instead.

You can do the same thing for upcoming vacations and other large bills you know are coming due in the future. It's nice to go on a vacation that is already paid for, not having to worry about a large credit card bill welcoming you when you get back.

As you become more experienced using the free online budgeting system, one feature you will find is *My Projects,* a super tool you can use to easily handle any non-monthly bill or project. We've dedicated most of Week 9 for this powerful tool. *My Projects* allows for a flexible reserve schedule, multiple payments, and easy adjustments as you go.

If you don't need that kind of power, you can also use our Irregular Payments calculator in the Budgeting Section of our website to determine how much money you need to set aside each month to meet your non-monthly payments as they come due as shown in Figure 4-3. The calculator assumes that you just paid each of these bills and you are now working to set aside money for the next time the bills comes due. This is a great tool when you have a number of non-monthly bills and need to figure out how much in total you need to save each month.

Irregular Payments Budget Calculator

This calculator will convert your non-monthly payments into their monthly equivalents, and then provide you with a total. This total will represent how much you will need to set aside each month in order to make your non-monthly payments as they come due. A great budgeting tool!

Memory Joggers >>> [Auto Insurance ▾]

Payment Description	# of Pmts Per Year	Amt of Each Pmt	Monthly Amount

[Calculate Results] [Clear Form]

Total amount you need to set aside each month in order to meet your non-monthly payments as they come due.

[Create Report]

FIGURE 4-3

FINANCIAL GOAL #4 – GETTING CAUGHT UP

I put Financial Goal #3 and #4 together because they are similar both in function and in importance. By preparing for large non-monthly bills before they come due, you are essentially getting caught up on those bills. Now I need you to consider all your other bills you habitually pay late. Those late fees and added interest can suck the life out of anyone's budget, so you need to get caught up on these and begin paying them on time or even a little early. By doing this, you will be relieving yourself of the stress of wondering whether someone is going to cut one of your utilities or repossess something you have worked so hard to obtain.

In order to take care of those bills past due, you will include a line in your budget for the normal monthly payment, and then you will add another line to show how much you are applying to that same bill to get caught up. You may not be able to catch all up in one month, but do what you can and you will eventually achieve your goal.

Many loans give you a grace period that usually allows you up to fifteen more days to pay before they whack you with a late fee. Don't think that you are on time if you are paying in this grace period. I want you paying this bill before the grace period starts. If you've been paying late at all, make sure you include the bill in your budget as an item that needs to be caught up.

FINANCIAL GOAL #5 – MUCH-NEEDED REPAIRS

If you are like me, you've got a "honey-do" list that's a mile long. If you've completed Financial Goals #1-4, you are now in a much better position to take care of some of those things you have been neglecting for a while. Some of these items could be pretty expensive, like a new set of tires to replace the bald ones currently on your car. How about that room that needs a new coat of paint? Or maybe a little landscaping work to bring up the value of your home? It could be that *you* are in need of some much-needed repairs. Has it been more than six months since you've seen a dentist for a cleaning because you don't have dental insurance? I would put that on your list to prevent some major expensive work that would be required due to improper dental care and treatment. How about that wart on your hand? Let's get that taken care of. I need you feeling good about yourself as you get closer and closer to achieving your goals. How about a relationship that is in need of repair? Spend a little money and send some flowers to that special someone, making them feel special again! How about your kids? Take some money and treat them to a night of fun!

FINANCIAL GOAL #6 – FREE MONEY

Sometimes, I wonder whether I should even include this particular item as a goal. I know what you are asking: why wouldn't everyone want some free money? Where do you go to get in line for such a treat? Many employers offer their employees matching money if they contribute to a 401K plan at work. Some will match whatever you contribute dollar for dollar up to a certain amount, usually controlled by the IRS. I hesitate only because I am uncertain what the government may do with this money in the near future. It is possible that some or all of what you have invested will be taken away to fund another government program. Add to that the uncertainty of the market and the headaches of trying to determine how to invest your retirement money, and now you have a not-so-appealing goal to undertake. Another consideration is that the money you put into your 401K is not liquid. It's not easy to tap into that money if you need some quick cash. There are restrictions, paperwork, penalties, and requirements to repay any amount you borrow from your 401K.

Having said all that, you still need to prepare for the future so that when you are old and grey, you'll have some money to live on. If your employer is willing to cough up some free money as you contribute to your 401K, I think you should make it one of your goals to try to maximize the amount they contribute. One way to accomplish this is to take a percentage of your raise each year and apply that toward your 401K. That way, you still get some of the benefit of your raise to help pay for the increase in cost of living, but the amount invested doesn't hurt your budget that much because it is money you have never seen. Keep doing this each year until you are receiving the company's maximum matching contribution. After you get to this point, you will then need to spend a little more time analyzing how much money you would like to have at retirement and determining how much extra money beyond the company's match you are willing to contribute, or choosing a different strategy to fund your retirement through other qualified or non-qualified plans. What's the difference between a qualified plan and a non-qualified plan? With a qualified plan, your contributions are tax deductible, meaning Uncle Sam will not charge you tax on the amount you contribute, UNTIL later. At the time of retirement, you are then charged tax on withdrawals at whatever tax bracket you happen to be in at that time. Basically, you are gambling that the tax bracket you are in at retirement is going to be less that what you are in during your contribution years. Keep in mind, that during your working years, you had deductions that probably kept your "effective tax" rate low, such as kids, college funding, mortgage interest, etc. At retirement, your "effective tax rate" may be considerably higher since you will likely not have these types of deductions. That's where a non-qualified retirement savings plan may be worth considering. You will need to seek the advice of a financial professional to determine viable options, as described later in financial goals #7 and #8.

FINANCIAL GOAL #7 – SHORT-TERM SUCCESS

You're doing great. You are really starting to manage your money well. You've got a little money in reserve, you've got your monthly bills caught up, you've taken care of some things you had previously neglected, you are preparing for retirement, and now you are ready to focus on getting rid of that debt. However, there are so many loans and so little time. Which one should you tackle first? I like to take care of the loans with the smallest balance first. If you can get these paid off, you eliminate a monthly bill, which gives you that much more money to apply to the next loan you are looking to pay off. Pay off two of them and your savings will really start to add up. Now more and more cash will be available to apply to the next larger loan. This strategy of paying off your loans is called the "domino or snowball strategy." You start off small, and as each loan is paid, you build momentum to pay off the next loan.

Use the Accelerated Debt Payoff calculator in the Dealing with Debt section to calculate how quickly your debt will be paid off when you use this strategy. Figure 4-4 is an example of someone that had three bills with a combined monthly payment of $223.00. By implementing this strategy, and adding an extra $50 per month, the results are astounding! We reduce the time it would have taken to pay off the three bills from 64 months to 37 months. That's over two years early! In addition, we saved over $500 in interest by paying early. Use the print options to create a payment schedule that you can use to keep track of how far you have progressed and to see what's left.

If you want to try to pay off all your bills in a certain number of months, simply adjust the extra amount you can apply each month until you have the results you are looking for. If you get off track for a few months, just run through the exercise again to get a fresh schedule.

Accelerated Debt Payoff Calculator (Debt Snowball)

This calculator will show you how much time and money you could save by paying off your debts using the "rollover" method (a.k.a debt snowball). Using the rollover method, as each smaller debt is paid off, the freed-up payment amount is then applied to the next larger debt, and so on until all debts are paid off. As you are about to see, the rollover method can save you a ton of money in interest charges, and get you debt free in a very short period of time.

		Entry Columns			Calculated Columns	
#	Creditor	Principal Balance ($)	Interest Rate (%)	Payment Amount ($)	Interest Cost	# of Pmts Left
1	Bill 1	500	5	35	$16.59	15
2	Bill 2	2500	8	75	$336.74	38
3	Bill 3	6000	7	113	$1,201.57	64
4						
5						
6						
7						
8						
9						
10						

Enter a monthly dollar amount you can add to your debt payoff plan: 50

Calculate Results Clear Form

Results	Principal Balance	Interest Rate	Payment Amount	Interest Cost	# of Pmts Left
Current totals:	$9,000.00	N/A	$223.00	$1,554.89	64
ADP totals:	$9,000.00	N/A	$273.00	$1,051.13	37
Time and interest savings from Accelerated Debt Payoff Plan:				$503.76	27

The total of your current monthly debt payments ($223.00), plus the additional monthly amount of $50.00, is equal to $273.00. This is how much you will allocate to paying off your debts until all of the above debts are paid off.

Create Payment Schedule Create Payoff Summary

FIGURE 4-4

In addition to paying off some of your smaller loans, you should now take a peek at some of your short-term purpose-driven goals, or even one of your short-term bucket list items. There's no reason why we can't get to work on some of these now. Also, an important item you should not overlook is life insurance. There are many types of life insurance products on the market and it can become quickly overwhelming trying to decide which product is right for you and trying to determine the right face amount – which is the amount the insurance company will pay to your beneficiaries in the event of your death. There are some that propose you should only shop for term life insurance, basically because it is so cheap as compared to other insurance products such as whole life or universal life insurance. In reality, the true cost of insurance regardless of type is regulated by the states and is primarily based on mortality tables, which define the life expectancy for various groups. With term insurance, the company will pay the "face-amount" of the policy ONLY if you die within the term, which is usually set at 10 or 20 years. After the term is up, you must buy it again, USUALLY at a higher price because the likelihood that you will die during the next term has increased based on the mortality tables, and the cost of inflation requires companies to charge more from one year to the next. Term insurance may actually be impossible to buy for those that are older because the premiums are so high and, when added up, will nearly equal the face amount of the policy. Do not be trapped into the thought that term insurance will always be cheaper. Compare term insurance with a simple whole life policy, where your premium is guaranteed to never go up, will never expire (as long as you pay premiums) and the policy will build cash-value over time. Sure, you may pay more during the beginning, but as you grow older, you cash value grows, your death benefit grows (with the cash value) but your premium remains the same from one year to the next. When you compare term insurance to other insurance like this, you can see you must take everything into consideration when determining whether you are getting the best deal. With term insurance, your health may have declined in the previous term making you uninsurable. You are not guaranteed you'll be able to renew term insurance after your existing policy expires. With permanent insurance, such as whole life or universal, your policy never expires as long as sufficient premiums are paid. Another benefit of permanent insurance is the living benefit riders available to many plans, such as a benefit to provide income due to a disability. Group term insurance provided by your company may be very appealing, but many times, you may be able to find it cheaper through an independent source since the insurance company looks at the group as a whole, and may charge a higher rate than what you would qualify for on your own.

Now that you are starting to get a good picture of your financial situation, I would recommend meeting with a licensed insurance professional to allow him or her to perform a confidential review of your finances and insurance needs. In the next financial goal #8, there are some strategies where your working reserves may be best handled through a combination of providing for your insurance needs along with methods to quickly build cash values that can be easily tapped into as needs arise.

FINANCIAL GOAL #8 – WORKING RESERVES

Now that you have paid off some of those small loans and your financial standing is improving, we need to build your personal reserves for greater contingencies. We need to make sure life-changing events don't negatively impact your finances, at least not for a while. One of the most common life-changing events is the loss of a job. All of a sudden, your income drops dramatically and all you are left with is an unemployment check. It's going to be extremely hard to maintain your current lifestyle if you do not have significant reserves on hand to tap. Ten years ago, I would have said you should have three to six months' worth of bring-home income as reserves. Today, the number of unemployed or underemployed workers is high, and it could take much longer to land a new job. Even if you are lucky enough to get hired, the pay may be less than you were previously earning, so it would be nice to have a large amount of reserves on hand so you can slowly acclimate your family to some lifestyle changes that correspond to your new earning power. As of right now, I recommend six to twelve months' worth of bring-home income in reserves. That's going to be a tremendous amount of money, usually several thousand dollars. As you can imagine, it may take several years to accumulate this kind of money, so this is something we will need to methodically tackle month after month.

As the money starts to build, what do you do with it? The first $5,000 in reserves I would leave in your checking account. These are your working reserves. Once you have achieved this level of success, you can start putting that $5,000 to work for you. How do you do that? First, let's look at your vehicle and home insurance policies. Most insurance policies require you to pay a deductible before the insurance company begins paying their portion of a claim. Usually, the lower the deductible, the higher the insurance premium is. Once you have $5,000 in reserves in your checking account, consider raising those deductibles to a much larger amount and enjoying the smaller premiums. Why pay the insurance company for the added protection of a low deductible when you can provide that protection yourself in the form of reserves? Isn't that what reserves are for anyway? Do this for all your property insurance policies. Just know that when a claim does occur, it will be your reserves that are tapped to apply to the larger deductible, and you will have to rebuild those reserves again if you do not have another form of savings to tap.

Another advantage of having $5,000 worth of reserves in your checking account is that they provide relief from a bad cash flow position. The $1,000 in "grand" reserves will help some, but $5,000 is better! For some people, many of their bills come due at the beginning of the month. Although they will have the money to pay the bills, they won't have it until they get paid later in the month, so they are forced to pay late. This is a bad cash flow position.

It's better to already have cash on hand when you start your budget so you can pay bills as they come due, regardless of what day of the month you get paid. Some companies only pay their employees once every two weeks or even once a month. Very few companies still pay on a weekly basis because of the amount of payroll overhead and expense to process paychecks on such a frequent basis. People who are retired or on disability are extremely susceptible to bad cash flow as they only get paid once a month. Having the money in reserve really helps out!

The disadvantage of having all that cash in your checking account is that it is sitting there earning zero interest, or at best, near zero. That's why, in financial goal #7, I recommended that you begin the process to meet with an independent financial professional that specializes in insurance so they can not only recommend the right amount of life insurance you need based on your current lifestyle, but can also recommend other products and riders that could potentially help you methodically build cash value reserves that are earning a decent amount of interest. One particular strategy allows you access to your cash reserves in the form of a low interest loan, leaving your accumulated cash value and interest untouched. This provides a way to finance future expenses at virtually zero interest (because the interest you are earning is near (or greater than) the interest you are paying on the loan). The other advantage to this strategy is compound interest is never reset on your cash value. You will not only continue to earn interest on your cash value, but will also continue to earn interest on the interest you earned (compounding). With other strategies, where cash is withdrawn, or CD's are cashed in, interest and compounding is reset back to the amount of remaining cash value. Please take a moment to discuss strategies like this with your life insurance professional to see if they have products like this that you may be able to take advantage of.

FINANCIAL GOAL #9 – THE LONG HAUL

If you have made it to this goal, you need to consider writing your own book, because you are a budget master. You are now financially able to consider those large and lofty goals that many would only dream of, such as paying cash for your child's college education or buying that new house or car or vacation home. There is nothing to stop you from achieving any remaining financial goals you might have.

The only suggestion I might make here is for you to take a close look at your charitable contributions. You should always consider your giving at any level, but at this stage, you have the opportunity to impact not just a few lives but many lives. Also, do not forget where you came from. Circumstances could change quickly and you might find yourself right back where you started. Take advantage of the opportunities to give while you still can.

WEEK 4 – QUESTIONS & DISCUSSION
(You may copy this page as needed)

1. What type of goals are achieved the easiest?

    _____

    _____

    _____

2. Why should you build a "cash stash" and "grand reserves" before taking care of bills that are paid late?

    _____

    _____

    _____

3. Name a few repairs you need to take care of. How much do you think they will cost?

    _____

    _____

    _____

4. TRUE or FALSE.
    When implementing the debt snowball strategy, you are only concerned with each bill's minimum payment required.

5. Which financial goal will be hardest for you to accomplish?

    _____

    _____

    _____

6. PRACTICE!
    Use the online Accelerated Debt Payoff calculator in the Dealing with Debt section to calculate how quickly your debt will be paid off, assuming you can add $50 extra per month.

WEEK 5 - MY INCOME

THE IMPRESSIONABLE YEARS

There is no denying that how we are raised has a huge effect on how we will act as adults. Think about how you handled money as a child. Did you get an allowance? Did you have to complete your chores before you were given that money? I believe my first allowance was a whole quarter a week. I don't remember having to do too much to earn that money, other than making my bed and picking up toys in my room. As I got older, I was assigned a portion of the yard that I had to mow, and I had to take out the trash to the trash barrel. That last job was fun because where I grew up, I could throw the trash into the barrel and then light it on fire! It was always fun watching the cans of hair spray and other flammables blow up. In the winter, it was even more fun throwing snow against the hot barrel and watching it sizzle. I think those memories are why I always love poking a campfire with a stick today. I think the chore I hated the most, though, was washing the dishes after dinner. That task seemed to take forever! Because of these chores, I learned early on that you didn't get money for doing nothing. If I was slack on doing my chores one week, my parents would let me know that if I didn't complete my work, there would be no allowance coming. Those threats always kept me motivated.

We had a little grocery store in town that I would visit to spend my allowance. I usually bought comic books, candy, or a can of soda. As I got older, I wanted more and more toys and "things". I don't know why I was so materialistic. I had a huge stamp collection, compiled from stamps I ordered from a mail order service or bought from the post office across the street. I then started work on my first model railroad. I loved trains. There was a train track that went through our town, and it was always fun counting the number of cars attached to the train as it went by. I realized at an early age that if you had the money, you could get just about anything. So, I went about doing everything I could to earn money with no purpose other than to obtain more stuff. I guess you could say I was a poster child for a capitalistic or materialistic kid.

In the summer time, I would mow the grass for some of the older folks in town. I'd usually make three to five dollars, and they would invite me in for a drink and chat with me for a while. It was fun talking with the older folks; they seemed happy just to have someone around. Other times, I would go pick some fresh wild raspberries from around the river and try to sell them to some of the other folks in town, but my mom usually ended up buying them from me. I would also get on my bike and ride through the countryside, picking up aluminum cans from the side of the road. Dad would take me to the recycling center, where they would pay me a little money for those aluminum cans. I thought it was the coolest thing, getting cash for trash! Looking back on it, I probably made only pennies an hour based on the amount of time I spent looking for the cans, dealing with the stench, emptying them out, crushing them, and storing them until I had enough cans to make a trip to the recycling center.

For a couple of years, I delivered newspapers, specifically the Indianapolis Star, to the folks in town. The Star wasn't the local paper so I only had a few customers, but I understood the dedication that was required, even to the point of having to deliver papers in sub-zero temperatures. One day, my dad insisted on driving me around because it was so cold, and one of his fingers ended up getting frostbitten. I didn't make much money delivering newspapers, but my district manager must have liked me because he gave me a trip to New York City for trying to get more customers signed up during the Star's paper drive contest. Thus, I learned there are rewards for hard work, even if you miss your goal. That trip to New York City was the trip of a lifetime! I got to go during Thanksgiving weekend and attend Macy's Thanksgiving Day Parade. It's amazing how times have changed. My parents put me on the bus with a ton of other kids and only a few chaperones who turned us loose on the streets during the parade. I was walking around all by myself along the parade route trying to get a better view of the floats. It was a little intimidating and scary looking up at all the tall buildings. I started to wonder where I was because all the buildings looked alike! It's a wonder I didn't get lost. One night, I walked down to the hotel lobby and asked a gentleman for a coke. He told me it would cost me $2.50, which was a lot of money for a little boy back in the 1970s. He then told me if I walked across the street to the convenience store, I could get a can of soda for only twenty-five cents. Of course, I ran across the street for the cheaper alternative. What an impression winning that trip made on me.

In the fall, I would rake leaves for the neighbors to make some more money. In the winter, it was shoveling snow. In the spring, it was time for yard sales and lemonade stands. Now that I think about it, I should have been a millionaire by the time I got out on my own based on the number of jobs I did! I was so consumed with finding money, I would dig holes in our backyard trying to find gold, digging some holes deeper than I was tall. I don't know why I thought I was going to find anything. I think it was because my dumb older brother told me that if I dug far enough, I would find gold. I never did, though, and I ended up having to put all the dirt back.

As I reached my teenage years, I started working on the farms. My first hourly paying job was baling hay for three dollars an hour. That led to helping out on the dairy farm I mentioned earlier, where I shoveled silage down from the high silage bin for the cows to eat, cleaned out manure-laden stalls with a pitch fork, and of course milked the cows. You all need to be thankful for

Louis Pasteur and the milk pasteurization process after what I saw and experienced milking cows. I told my old boss how hard this work was, and he replied that hard work builds character. I look back now and have to agree. Hard work like that taught me never to give up, to keep moving forward, and to be grateful for what I have. I was able to save $600 my senior year in high school by working on the farm, and I used that money to pay cash for my first car. It was a jacked-up 1972 Ford Mach I Mustang. The car may sound impressive, but you get what you pay for. The car was a rust bucket. I could actually see the road beneath my feet as I was driving because rust had chewed a hole through the floorboard. I took comfort in the fact that if the engine died, I could always push the car *Flintstones* style. On one trip into town, the engine suddenly died, so I pulled over. The straps holding the gas tank in place had rusted through, and the gas tank had fallen off. My dad came to the rescue, threw some boards in the trunk, and chained the tank back into position. I was still grateful for my car, though, because it was something I had paid for, and I did everything I could to keep it on the road.

By looking at my childhood, you can see there were many experiences that shaped the way I handle money today. Most of these experiences were positive, while some were not. I did learn to appreciate the value of a dollar, what it took to earn one, and how to take care in spending it. Take a moment and think about your childhood experiences and how certain events shaped the way you handle money today.

CAREERS

How does your current career line up with the goals you have? Does the job you have today provide for even the basic necessities? The job you have now may not even be the dream job you had hoped for when you were a child. I took a career test when I was in high school, and when the results came back, I was really disappointed to see what I had received. To my dismay, I was told I would make an excellent secretary because of how fast I was able to answer the questions. Clearly, a secretarial position was not the dream job I had hoped for. However, I did not let those tests distract me from my dream job of working with computers. After my little stint in the manufacturing arena (the one that ended in a mauled arm), I made the decision to head to a technical college and get my degree in computer technology so that I could become a computer programmer.

I think it is becoming increasingly difficult for young people to understand how careers work. Most likely, you'll have to start out at the bottom of the ladder, just like everyone else. I landed my first computer-related job as a computer operator, making what I thought was good money at $5.25 an hour. I was happy in what I was doing, and this was my opportunity to get my foot in the door so I could possibly move into a computer programming position. That's exactly what happened. After a short while, I was hired as a computer programmer, giving me the chance to build my skills and make more and more money. A career is something you have to stick with and build over many years. You have to have a passion for the field in which you are working. With some careers, it's not going to be about the money, but rather about enjoying what you do and making your mark in this world, making a difference for those around you and those you love.

MEASURING YOUR WORTH

So how much do you think you are worth? I know when I was growing up, my parents told me I was worth a million dollars! Actually, they told me they wouldn't sell me, even for a million dollars. I have seen lawsuits where someone is injured in an automobile accident and can no longer continue the work they were doing due to injuries they received. The party who caused the accident is usually sued for the amount of money that the injured person would have earned during their remaining working years, or the number of months or years they are unable to work. Is that how a person's worth is measured, by the amount of money they could have earned in their lifetime?

Measuring your real net worth from time to time is actually a valuable exercise you will want to do in order to document how your financial condition changes over time. Before you start you first budget, you may want to calculate your net worth to set a baseline that can be used to gauge how well your budget is helping you improve your net worth. Use the Net Worth calculator in the Budgeting section to calculate your net worth. See Figure 5-1.

This calculator is designed to help you to take a "picture" of your current financial condition. Whereas an income and expense statement (your budget) shows you your financial picture for a period of time (month, year, etc.), this calculator will show you your financial picture at a single point in time (a specific date). That way, if you compute your Net Worth now, and then again 3 months from now, you will be able to tell whether your financial picture is improving or getting worse. Use the print feature to print a copy for future comparison.

Net Worth Calculator

This calculator was designed to help you to take a "picture" of your current financial condition. Whereas an income and expense statement (your budget) shows you your financial picture for a period of time (month, year, etc.), this Net Worth Calculator will show you your financial picture at a single point in time (a specific date). That way, if you compute your Net Worth now, and then again 3 months from now, you will be able to tell whether your financial picture is improving or getting worse.

Your Name		◈ Enter date to display on report	
Assets		◈ **Liabilities**	
Liquid Assets		◈ *Short-Term*	
Cash (checking & savings accounts)		◈ Credit Cards	
Short-Term Investments		◈ Car Loan	
Treasury Bills		◈ Construction Liens/Notes/Balances Due	
Savings Certificates		◈ Loan on Life Insurance	
Money Market Funds		◈ Installment Loans	
Cash Value of Life Insurance		◈ Accrued Income Taxes	
Other		◈ Other Debt	
Total Liquid Assets		◈ **Total Short-Term Liabilities**	
Investment Assets		◈ *Long-Term*	
Notes Receivable		◈ Loans to Purchase Personal Assets	
Marketable Securities		◈ Loan to Acquire Business	
Securities		◈ Mortgage on Personal Residence(s)	
Bonds		◈ Note to Business	
Real Estate (investment)		◈ Other	
Tax Incentive Investments		◈ Other	
Retirement Funds		◈ Other	
Total Investment Assets		◈ **Total Long-Term Liabilities**	
Personal Assets		◈ *Contingent Liabilities*	
Residence		◈ Endorser	
Vacation Property		◈ Guarantor (SBA Loan)	
Art, Antiques		◈ Damage Claims	
Furnishings		◈ Taxes	
Vehicles		◈ Other	
Other		◈ Other	
Total Personal Assets		◈ **Total Contingent Liabilities**	
Total Assets		◈ **Total Liabilities**	
		Net Worth	

Printer Friendly Report | Clear Form

FIGURE 5-1

For income's sake, most are measured by how much money they are making per hour. Many times, that amount fluctuates greatly based on whether you are an hourly employee or a salaried employee. Hourly employees are usually paid less per hour, but they have the advantage of making more money for overtime hours, and even more for working holidays. Therefore, the amount they make per hour can increase if they are given the opportunity. A salaried employee is paid a fixed amount of income regardless of the number of hours they work. I have seen some people who appear to make a good salary, but when I ask them how many hours they had to work, their answer is usually more than forty. Every extra hour the employee works above that number effectively decreases the amount of money he or she makes per working hour, so if you are a salaried person, the amount you make per hour will normally decrease if you need to put in extra work to get your job done.

Sometimes I wonder whether people really consider their worth. Take a married couple with a few pre-school kids, for example. The parents want to get back to work as soon as they can, so they send the kids off to daycare. If they were to take the amount charged per hour for someone to watch those kids, deduct it from the amount they make per hour, and take a look at what's left, they would likely see that a good portion of their salaries is being used to pay for the gas to get to work, as well as all the other expenses that come with maintaining a job (clothes, vehicle maintenance, etc.). However, there is a catch if one of them decides not to go back to work but to be a stay-at-home parent. If the parent decides to stay at home with the kids until they reach school age, he or she risks the possibility of not being able to find another job or losing the skills or certifications for his or her current position. If you are facing this decision, my advice would be to take a step back, consider your long-term goals, and discern what purpose you have to continue to work. For some, that will mean making a short-term sacrifice and continuing to work. For others, it may mean it's time to change direction. There is no right or wrong answer here; it's simply something to consider.

Perhaps you are paid solely on a commission basis, or maybe you work mainly for tips. Others of you may work seasonally, fluctuating between times of feast and famine. These types of jobs can make budgeting really difficult because you never know how much money you are bringing home each week. It will take some discipline during the times of feasting for you to set aside some of that money for later, when the times of famine hit. If you can at least reach the financial goal of having working reserves on hand, you'll be in a much better position to bring balance to your rollercoaster of paychecks. Getting to that point is going to be extremely hard, because when you come out of famine mode, there is always so much you need to spend your money on. Everyone in the family is chirping like little birds with their mouths wide open, waiting to hear the magic word . . .

PAYDAY!

Payday! Everyone loves to hear that word. The mere mention of payday instantly transforms the average man or woman into a shopping fanatic. After the gluttonous spending is completed, buyer's remorse sets in and the state of mind changes from euphoria to depression. The person still has another week before next payday if he or she is lucky, but maybe two weeks or even a month! You don't need to live like this. There is a better way.

First, let's get the definition of "income" right. We can break this word down into two simple syllables: "In" and "come." In other words, let the money come in before it burns a whole in your pocket and you spend it all. There is nothing more depressing than to receive your paycheck on one day and to be broke the very next day. A little self-control and discipline will be needed to avoid engaging in impulse buying. Impulse buying ends up creating many unbudgeted entries that will make maintaining your budget a much more difficult experience.

If you are married and have been previously forbidden to touch the other's paycheck, now is the time to consider pooling your money to get a clearer picture of your overall financial position. If you meet resistance, you may need to help your spouse understand what you are trying to accomplish and even make more allowances in their favor for the time being.

EASY MONEY

If you are struggling to make ends meet, you have two choices. You can either increase your income or decrease your expenses until your income is greater than, or at least equal to, your total expenses. It sounds like an easy concept, but if you watch the news, you can see how difficult a time the government has as they try to accomplish this simple mathematical miracle. The reason for this struggle is because such a task is rife with political opinions regarding what is the best way to bring in more income and what expenses should be cut. In *Week 7 - My First Budget*, we'll talk in more detail about the proper approach to identifying expenses that can be cut. For now, though, we'll concentrate on finding ways we can increase income.

Let's start with your paycheck. You are paid a whole lot more than you actually bring home, unless you are one of the few employees who are paid in cash for some reason. Grab a copy of your paystub and look at all the deductions made to your gross income. Some are statutory, which means you are forced to pay, while others are voluntary. You'll see deductions such as federal income tax, social security, state tax, health insurance, life insurance, 401K, company stock purchase plan, Christmas club, etc. etc. Just take a look at all the deductions listed on this sample paycheck in Figure 5-2.

Deductions   Statutory

Federal Income Tax

Social Security Tax

Medicare Tax

SC State Income Tax

Other

Checking

Dental

Flex Med Acct

Medical

Supp Life Emp .

Supp Life Spous

Supp - Ad&D - Emplo

Supp - Life - Child

Charity Special

Ee Store

Stock

Stock Match

FIGURE 5-2

Wouldn't it be nice to eliminate all of those deductions and keep all the money you actually earn? Unfortunately, there is nothing we can do about some of those, but we can decide whether or not we want to decrease the amount going toward many of these and thus effectively *increase* our take-home income. Your federal income tax is a statutory deduction and is based on the number of allowances you have claimed on the W4 form you had to fill out when you started your employment. Many people make the mistake of simply entering the number of deductions, or number of individuals in the family, as the number of allowances on the form. Normally, however, this amount is too low, which means that most families are having more money withheld from their paycheck than necessary. These families then receive a large tax refund from the government each year because they have overpaid. Basically, they have given the government an interest-free loan for the year. Sure, they will pay back the money next year, but only if the families can prove the money is theirs, and of course, no one earns any interest on a loan to the government.

The purpose of the W4 form is to estimate how much you will need to pay in taxes based on your salary, dependents, and estimated deductions for the coming year. Many people are confused about the form and think if they enter more allowances than the number of dependents they have, the IRS is going to come audit them. Others don't want to take the time to fill out the form correctly (because it does take planning), especially since the payroll department asks them to fill it out and turn it in on their first day on the job, leaving them no time to plan. The good news is that you can change your W4 allowances at any time. Ask your payroll department for an updated form and take the time to fill it out properly. In my case, the W4 form told me I should claim eight allowances based on my circumstances, even though I only have two kids and a wife. I still received a sizable refund each year, so I increased the number again. Ask yourself whether or not you get a federal tax refund each year and how much it is. If it is a substantial amount, consider going to the payroll department and filling out a new W4 form with an increased number of deductions.

Many websites exist that allow you to enter the information from your paystub and then play with different variables to see what impact that has on your paycheck. One particular website (www.paycheckcity.com) even has a W4 form calculator and will print out the W4 form for your payroll department. Be careful, though; many families have become dependent on their annual tax refunds to pay for certain large expenses. Just be aware that if you increase your allowances on the W4 form, you will receive more take-home pay and a smaller tax refund than previous years. Also, be careful not to go too far with your W4 allowances. If you don't pay enough taxes during the year, depending on the amount, you might have to pay the IRS a penalty for underpayment. It's generally a good idea to update your W4 whenever you have a major change in your life. That change could be anything from having children to buying a house to getting a new job; in short, anything that increases or decreases your deductions for the year.

What other kind of deductions do you see in your paycheck? Do you have a 401K deduction? I previously listed five goals that come before contributing money to your 401K fund, in my opinion. If you still have some work to do on any of those goals, seriously consider stopping those 401K contributions, at least until you are in better financial shape. I also don't recommend getting a loan from your 401K because you would be borrowing from Peter to pay Paul, only with interest.

Check your other deductions to see if they make sense and if they are the right amount. Question everything! You've worked hard for that money. Some people believe that if you don't see it, you'll never miss it, but money is money, for crying out loud! If you are a single adult with a million dollar term life insurance deduction, I'd say that's a good item to put on the chopping block. Don't be frivolous with your money just because you can be.

In my previous job, the company would allow me to charge my lunch at the company cafeteria, and they would deduct the money from my paycheck to cover the cost. I would get paid, and when my wife asked where all the money went, I would have to confess and say I ate high on the hog that pay period. Eating out, even at work, can add up to some serious money. Pack a lunch, keep the money in your paycheck, and increase your bring-home pay.

Another problem I had in a previous job was making purchases at the company store. It was so convenient, and the merchandise was so cheap. The problem was that I was using my paycheck like a credit card and making purchases I didn't need and couldn't afford. Unless it is both a real steal and something you actually need, stay away from the company store and keep the money in your paycheck.

Insurance plans are getting really complicated, and it is becoming more and more difficult for the average person to make informed decisions about how much to contribute to things like a Flexible Spending Account (FSA). FSAs are great because you get all the money for the year up front to pay for your medical expenses, prescriptions, and other approved items. They are also beneficial because you are not charged taxes on the money deducted from your paycheck to pay for them. That allows you to purchase FSA-approved goods tax free. However, there are a few catches here as well. If you don't spend all the money in your FSA account that year, the unspent money is lost. Also, it can be difficult to estimate exactly how much money you should put in your FSA because your circumstances will change from year to year. You may have had a bad year with many doctor visits and related expenses, but that's no indication that the coming year will be as bad or that it won't be worse. Your goal should be to try to put in just enough for or a little less than the expenses you expect to have. Then rely on your cash stash or reserves to cover unplanned expenses that come at the end of the year after your account has been depleted. If you have money left in your FSA account and you are facing the end of the year, you are forced to consider making a purchase for an FSA-approved item or procedure that you don't really need. I had over $300 left one year, and I was forced to buy a ton of Band-Aids and other health items I didn't need at the time. In a way, that's just as bad as impulse buying. Take some time to analyze your medical expenses over the past years before deciding whether to establish an FSA account and how much to put into it. You may be better off keeping that money in your paycheck, increasing your bring-home income.

As a side note, if an FSA is not an option for you, you might want to consider a Health Savings Account (HSA) to help cover some of the cost of your medical expenses if you are covered under an HSA-eligible high deductible plan. HSAs belong to you, not your employer, and allow you to roll over your balance from one year to the next. You can even withdraw funds from your HSA (although you are penalized if you do so before retirement). If you company does not sponsor an HSA, your contributions have to be made on a post-tax basis, but you can still claim this as a deduction on your 1040 form.

What are some other ways to bring in more income? One thing I like to do is check the weekly mail flyers for coupons. I'm not as fanatical as some, but I will and do use coupons whenever I can. They are spent just as easily as cash and are therefore a potential source of income. Some people maintain organized folders of coupons and have a list of websites they visit regularly to find the best deals. If you invest enough time, you can save a lot of money. The reason I don't go as far as others with coupons, however, is because it can take a long time to search for and to organize the coupons you need. In my experience, the value I get by searching for them isn't worth it. How much time do I need to spend doing all of that when I have other things I need to be doing? Still, others enjoy coupon-clipping, having fun trying to get their grocery bill down to zero!

You can also sign up for credit card rewards. If you can ever get to the point of getting your credit card paid off, you could use it for everyday purchases and budget the right amount to pay it off each month. By doing this, you can quickly earn various rewards. Some credit cards will actually let you redeem your points for cash. In short, you use your credit card to make purchases, you pay it off at the end of the month, and the credit card company pays you for using their card. They don't mind paying you because they are getting their money from the businesses that process your transactions. The danger here is in not properly budgeting the right amount to pay off the credit card during the month. If you spend too much, you may not have enough money to pay it off, and then your balance rolls over to the next month and you are charged interest for that balance. This could easily spiral out of control if not managed properly. I only recommend using your credit card in this way if you have lived on a budget for a number of months, if you can provide a good estimate on what you'll be putting on that credit card, and if you have some reserves built up in case you do go over the amount in your budget.

The methods I have described above are relatively easy ways to increase your income. If you are still struggling to make ends meet, you should look at the easy ways to decrease expenses as described next week. For now, I'll continue to list the more difficult ways to earn some extra money.

LIQUIDATION

After considering the easy ways to earn some extra money, I would look through my house for things to sell that I no longer need or use. You may want to consider having a yard sale, or if some of the items are more valuable, you might post the item on an auction site like e-Bay or Craig's List. It's hard to get even a fraction of the amount you originally paid for an item, so if there is a chance the item could be useful in the future, you might want to keep it. Pawn shops are notorious for giving you a rock bottom price for your treasures, so try to find a buyer on your own first. Depending on the price of gold and silver, now may be a good time to sell your scrap jewelry. Any money you receive from these activities should be dedicated toward your initial goals.

REFINANCING

I hate refinancing. I've done it several times, and I hated doing it each time. It is such a hassle trying to pull together all the paperwork and to find the right lender who's not going to rob you blind with hidden fees. Then you go through the appraisal process, hoping your house is worth more than you owe. If your appraisal is positive, then your loan application goes to the underwriters, who determine whether or not you are a good risk and whether they will approve you for a loan. It is a stressful period as you progress from one step of the process to the next. However, refinancing may be a good move on your part if you are currently paying an interest rate higher than average. You could even end up getting some much-needed cash so that you can pay off debt or get caught up on overdue bills. Even if you don't have any equity you want to take out of the house, you could still earn some cash when you refinance because you normally get to skip a month before having to make your first payment, and you'll usually get a check in the mail from whatever escrow balance you had with your old mortgage company. You should therefore consider refinancing as a potential source of income.

Consider the following true story from John Gibson, owner of Summit Advisory Group. "Our client was pursuing the strategy to pay off his mortgage early. At age 35, he was following others advice and had been paying 2 times his mortgage payment. Unfortunately, he had a stroke and became totally disabled. When he and his wife went to the bank trying to get the equity out of their house to use to live, you guessed it, no loan for THEIR equity. They had to sell the house to get the money. If they had saved the money in another account they could have chosen to pay off the mortgage when there was enough money, or used it to live given the actual circumstances. I understand the psychological reasons for wanting the mortgage paid off, but rarely does it make the best financial sense."

Trying to figure out whether refinancing is the right move for you can be a daunting task. You could really make a mess of things if you don't do it right, so you need to seek the advice of a lending specialist or other competent professional before you start. If you insist on figuring things out on your own, use the Mortgage Refinance calculator in the Loans Part 2 section to help you decide whether or not you should refinance your current mortgage at a lower interest rate. See Figure 5-3. Not only will this calculator calculate the monthly payment and net interest savings, but it will also calculate how many months it will take to break even on the closing costs.

Mortgage Refinancing Calculator

This calculator will help you to decide whether or not you should refinance your current mortgage at a lower interest rate. Not only will this calculator calculate the monthly payment and net interest savings, but it will also calculate how many months it will take to break even on the closing costs.

Enter the principal balance of your mortgage: (call your mortgage lender and ask for the current payoff amount)	150000
Enter the amount of your monthly mortgage payment (Principal & Interest Only):	997.96
Enter your mortgage's current interest rate:	6.5
Enter interest rate you will be refinancing at:	4
Enter the number of years you will be refinancing for:	30
Enter the closing costs [percentage points ▾]: (Typically, # of points is "2" or dollar amount is .02 times the principal)	2
Would you like to finance the closing costs?	No ▾
Compute Reset	
This is how much your monthly payment will be if you refinance:	$716.12
Monthly Payment Reduction:	$281.84
# of months for interest savings to offset closing costs:	10
This is how much interest you will pay under your current monthly payment plan:	$160,890.27
This is how much interest you will pay under your refinanced monthly payment plan:	$107,805.25
This is how much interest you will save if you refinance:	$53,085.02
Net Refinancing Savings (interest savings less closing costs):	$50,085.02

If you refinance your current 6.50% mortgage to a 4.00% mortgage, your monthly payment will decrease by $281.84 and you will save $53,085.02 in interest charges over the life of the mortgage. However, in order for this refinancing to yield any savings at all you will need to stay in your current home for at least 10 months. That's how long it will take for the monthly interest savings to offset the closing costs attributable to refinancing.

FIGURE 5-3

If you do want to refinance, consider the number of years on your loan. Many would advise refinancing from a 30-year to a 15-year loan if you can afford the monthly payments to reduce the interest you have to pay. That may sound like a good strategy because of the equity that will also be quickly built in your home. In reality, however, that is most likely not the best strategy.

Consider the following facts. A family has a $300,000 home, qualify for a 4% interest rate, and is trying to determine whether it is better to refinance at 15 years or 30 years. Using a 15-year loan, at year 5, they would have nearly $81 thousand in equity, and at year 15, their home is paid for. What advantages would present themselves if they chose to refinance at a 30-year loan? If they took the extra cash from the lower payment and invested it with an expected rate of return of 4% as well, at the end of year 5, they would only have $29 thousand in equity, but would have cash plus earnings of $52 thousand, for a total of $81 thousand as well. If they earned 6%, they would have nearly $84 thousand. At year 15 at 6%, they now have $106 thousand in equity, and $229 thousand in cash and earnings, for a total of $335 thousand. So, at the end of year 15, they too can pay off the house, plus have $35 thousand left over! What other advantages do you realize with a strategy like this? You will enjoy larger tax deductions from additional mortgage interest paid, easy access to equity in times of emergencies (does not require you to sell house or get a second mortgage to get equity). If you were to tie this with an insurance product that allows you to build cash value over time, you will also enjoy tax-free earnings, equity protection for beneficiaries (by avoiding probate), and the possibility of a variety of other living benefits described earlier in our financial goals section. If you still decide to go forward from a 30-year to a 15-year loan, you need to consider how this might affect the deductions you claim each year and whether you need to update your W4 form with your employer. I was able to refinance to a ridiculously low interest rate once, and I noticed that a good portion of my monthly payment was going toward principle, while just a little was going toward interest. That was great, but it also meant the deductions I claimed each year on the 1040 form were reduced dramatically. I had to adjust my W4 to increase the amount of taxes taken out of my paycheck to make up the difference. Either way, it's best to seek the advice of a qualified professional before making a decision.

YOUR SECOND JOB

If you have cut all the expenses you can or you want to jump start your progress on your goals, then you might want to consider getting a second job. For some families, this is already a way of life. I wouldn't recommend living this way for a long period of time, though, as the number of hours spent working will surely take its toll on your body, mind, spirit, family, and friends.

Your second job should be something you enjoy doing, something that's low stress, and something that comes with decent pay to make it worthwhile. If overtime is available in your primary job, I would ask for it before looking for a second job (assuming you like what you are doing). Also, check with your company to make sure they are supportive of your desire to work at another job to supplement your income. You may have signed an agreement when you started work stating that you promise not to moonlight while employed at the company. Don't risk your current job. Your employers may be particularly sensitive to your moonlighting if you are seeking work in the same field in which you are currently employed. You could end up working for a competitor and not even realize it, which would definitely cause a conflict of interest. Just be open and honest with your employer and let them know what you are planning to do. If you are able to work a second job in the same field, use that opportunity to increase your skills so that you can take them back to your primary employer. Perhaps your boss will notice your increased productivity and skills and give you a raise so you don't have to work a second job!

JUST FOR FUN

There are many more ways to make money than the few I've listed here. Use your imagination! I went to visit my brother one time in California, and he took me gold panning to see if we could strike it rich. I was excited at the thought of finding a huge gold nugget worth thousands of dollars. Worse, I was actually finding some nice gold flakes and starting to get gold fever. All those flakes put together were no bigger than a small drop of water, but if I hadn't had anything better to do, I could have stayed out there forever. It was a lot of fun, though; definitely a much better experience than digging large holes in the backyard trying to find gold.

In my never-ending quest to strike it rich quick, I bought my brother's metal detector and continued my search for treasure. This was a little more adventurous, as I went from place to place, digging into the ground. However, this time was different because I had technology on my side. I took it to the beach with me one year and found a huge gold class ring. However, the person's name was inscribed on the inside and he happened to live in the same town as me some 260 miles away from the beach. He sure was a happy camper when I called him to tell him I had found his ring. I did find plenty of old coins and a ton of bottle caps, but I gave up the hobby when the police chased me away from a school yard. People just didn't seem to appreciate the free irrigation and core aeration I was providing as I dug up my treasures.

WRITING IT DOWN

Now that you have exhausted all sources of income, get out a piece of paper and write down the income you believe you can bring in this month. Unless it's a sure thing, don't include it. No matter how small, write it down, even if it is only a few dollars from your interest-bearing checking account. You'll use this information later as you create your actual budget.

WEEK 5 – QUESTIONS & DISCUSSION
(You may copy this page as needed)

1. Did you get an allowance as a child? If so, how did you spend it?

   _____

   _____

   _____

2. PRACTICE! Use the online Net Worth calculator in the Budgeting section to determine your current net worth. Write the amount down in space provided.

   _____

3. PREPARE! Obtain the most recent copy of your pay stub. Review current exemptions/allowances and deductions. Are there any that should be adjusted?

   _____

   _____

   _____

4. Name 3 ways you can bring in extra income.

   _____

   _____

   _____

5. PREPARE! Write down each source of income you have, along with the estimated amount and date you expect that income will be deposited or made available to you.

   _____

   _____

   _____

   _____

   _____

   _____

   _____

WEEK 6 - MY BILLS

I hate bills. Sometimes I wonder what it would be like to live totally off the grid and not have a single bill to have to worry about ever again. To be self-sufficient in all ways is a goal I hope to achieve one day, but that's going to be a really tall order to fill. Our pioneering ancestors of just a century or so ago had no problem whatsoever with self-sufficiency. If they needed power, they would go chop some more wood. If they needed groceries, they would grow it, hunt it, or raise it. Transportation was provided by horses, donkeys, and mules. If they couldn't obtain something on their own, they would trade for it. Their focus was not on living a debt-free lifestyle, but on survival. For most of us, survival is not really a problem. Even if you've had the worst luck in the world, you would be a rare case in today's society to struggle for survival. You might see the homeless on the side of the road, begging to work for food. Unfortunately for people who are actually poor, the majority of these folks choose that way of life because it is easy and they don't have to do anything for money other than stand by the side of the road. It's almost impossible to tell those who are truly in need from the professional beggars who are doing this for a living.

Most of us focus on living a debt-free lifestyle, but to be realistic, I know I'll never be able to rid myself of all bills. I'm always going to have those everyday living expenses and utilities. You probably have those as well, including a mortgage payment, car payment, and several credit card payments.

This week will separate the men from the boys and the women from the girls. Be an adult and face the reality of all the bills you have. In order to defeat an enemy, you must first know who your enemy is. How can you expect to defeat the enemy of debt until you take the time to get to know him and where he is coming from? This is not a passive enemy; he will not leave you alone, he can't be reasoned with, and he absolutely will not stop until you are broke! The only thing that can stop this creature is the power of the budget. You have done the easy part, writing down all your sources of income. Now let's start writing down all your expenses.

A bill is anything you have to pay for using the cash in your pocket, a check, your debit or credit card, or an automatic deduction from your account. Our goal is to eliminate as many bills as possible and to simplify the process of keeping track of what's left. Just as we did for income, we can start off by looking at your paycheck stub to see where your bills begin. Go back and review that part of *Week 5 - My Income* to confirm you have done all you can to reduce or eliminate some of these bills that come directly out of your paycheck before you even see the first dime. Next, go back through your checkbook or bank statement for the last couple of months and start writing down each type of bill you have had and the maximum amount you paid during that time. You'll be surprised by the number of bills you actually have.

Some of the more common bills are for power, phone, cable, cell phone, car payment, house payment or rent, groceries, eating out, gas, credit cards, and personal loans. Don't forget about car insurance and taxes. Try to not forget anything! Write it all down.

When you start your budget at budgetsteward.com, we will provide you with a template that you can use to select common expenses. After reviewing this long list, you can begin to understand why a budget is so important to count the real cost of making a living. How many of the below bills do you have?

Giving - Church
Giving - Charitable Organizations
Giving - Christmas Gifts
Housing - Mortgage - 1st
Housing - Mortgage - 2nd
Housing – Telephone
Housing - Bug Man
Housing – Internet
Housing - Homeowners Insurance
Housing – Rent
Housing - Renters Insurance
Housing – Satellite or Cable TV
Housing - HOA fees
Housing - Property Taxes
Housing – Trash
Housing – Netflix
Housing - Cell Phones
Transportation - Car Payment 1
Transportation - Car Payment 2
Transportation - Car Insurance
Transportation - Car Taxes/Tags
Transportation - Gas / Diesel
Transportation - Car Repairs
Transportation - Oil Change
Transportation – Other
Food – Groceries
Food - Dining Out
Food - School Lunches
Food – Other
Clothing – Children
Clothing – Adults

Clothing – Other
Debt - Credit Card 1
Debt - Credit Card 2
Debt - Credit Card 3
Debt - Student Loan 1
Debt - Student Loan 2
Debt – Furniture
Debt – Other
Personal - Health Insurance
Personal - Life Insurance
Personal - Child Care
Personal – Alimony
Personal - Child Support
Personal – Vacation
Personal - Income Taxes
Personal - Date Night
Personal - Cell Phone
Personal - Medical Bill
Personal - Spending Money
Personal - Satellite Radio
Personal - Health Club
Personal – Prescriptions
Personal – Entertainment
Personal – Other
Saving - Retirement Fund
Saving - College Fund
Saving - Emergency Buffer Fund
Saving - New Furniture Fund
Saving - Known Upcoming Expenses
Saving - New Car Fund
Saving - Wedding Fund

THE ART OF NEGOTIATION

Now that you have your preliminary list of bills in front of you, look at the maximum amount you have paid for each of those bills. Do you think you are getting a good deal, paying a fair price? Many families are beginning to do away with their home phones and simply rely on cell phones to remain in contact with the world. I've kept my landline home phone because it has better reception and is more convenient to access. However, I felt I was paying way too much per month for my landline phone, so I called the phone company to negotiate a lower price. Armed with some information to back up my claim that I was being overcharged, I explained to them I was receiving solicitations from the cable company to switch to their Internet-based phone for a fraction of what I was currently paying. I also explained to them I was considering cutting off the phone line entirely using only cell phones. I told them I liked having a phone line for the quality signal and convenience, but I could not justify the price I was currently paying and asked them kindly if there was anything they could do before I made a decision one way or the other. They offered to cut my phone bill in half if I would remain a customer, and I agreed. Having successfully negotiated for my lower price, I did the same for my satellite TV service, explaining to them that while I appreciated their customer service and quality channels, I was getting offers from others at a much cheaper rate. In reply, they offered to give me a discount for twelve months and asked me to call back at the end of that year to keep the discount going.

I know it's a pain to call and go through all the options before you actually get to talk with a real person, but we are talking about real money and real savings here. In my example, I spent thirty minutes on the phone and saved $30 a month on the phone bill alone. If I were to translate that effort into an hourly rate for the year, that would be the equivalent of earning $720 an hour! I'll work at that rate anytime! Don't be lazy, and don't be afraid to negotiate for a lower price.

Some of your bills may not be so easily changed, like your mortgage payment. You've already signed a contract and agreed to pay so much monthly until the debt is paid in full. The only ways to change your agreement are to pay it off or to refinance. As I said before, you should be careful if you choose the second option. You may be paying an extremely high interest rate right now, and refinancing could give you the opportunity to lower that interest rate. However, try not to start your mortgage payment over at the same number of years you used to have. If anything, refinance for a lower number of years. Use online resources to look at your amortization chart and see how much you'll be paying in interest and in principle on each payment and over the life of the loan. There are many variables to consider, such as whether you plan on staying in the house for a long time or for just a few years. Try to negotiate who pays for the appraisal, when the first payment comes due, and how many points you have to pay. Don't be afraid to be bold and make them tell you if they cannot do something.

Also, do not be hasty when signing a contract. Don't let the person you are working with sit there waiting for you to sign the contract while you are reading it. Instead, tell him or her you would like some time to review the contract and that you'll be in touch once you have made a decision. You'll need that time to read the fine points of your contract. I have seen many home improvement contractors who make it sound as though you are just an ant on the hill and they couldn't care less whether you accept their contract or not. Be especially wary if the people you hire seem to think they are doing you a favor or tell you that you need to sign quickly because their calendars are filling up. Always remember, the customer is always right, and if they tell you that you are not right, you should tell them you are not their customer. It's your money, and you are the boss.

You'll want to make sure every detail that could impact your lifestyle is considered. For example, do you have a clause in the contract that tells the workers they need to complete the job in so many days and what reduced rate goes into effect if they don't? I've had contractors out at my house much longer than I wanted, and I felt they should have finished the job long ago. If you do not want a live-in contractor, make sure you spell out in the contract when the job needs to be finished and what the penalties are for missing the deadline. You also need to spell out when payments will be made. If at all possible, make no payments until the job is done. That's their incentive to finish and finish well. Make sure you have a warranty period specified, as well as the method to request work that falls under warranty and the time frame for them to respond to your claim. Make sure the work covered under the warranty is clear. If appropriate, ask for references and a copy of their insurance. Negotiate for everything!

FINANCIAL GOALS

Now that you have written down all the bills you know of and may have negotiated some of them to a lower price, let's work through the list of financial goals and get them on the list of expenses as well. We want them on the list even if we are not going to be able to put any money toward all of them yet, especially since we need to remember what we are working toward. Let's recap what those financial goals were.

FINANCIAL GOAL #1 – YOUR CASH STASH
FINANCIAL GOAL #2 – YOUR "GRAND" RESERVES
FINANCIAL GOAL #3 – LARGE RECURRING HEADACHES
FINANCIAL GOAL #4 – GETTING CAUGHT UP
FINANCIAL GOAL #5 – MUCH-NEEDED REPAIRS
FINANCIAL GOAL #6 – FREE MONEY
FINANCIAL GOAL #7 – SHORT-TERM SUCCESS
FINANCIAL GOAL #8 – WORKING RESERVES
FINANCIAL GOAL #9 – THE LONG HAUL

You may only be able to work on the first financial goal this month, but you need to keep the others in mind so you know in which direction you are heading. There's no need to write down the amount you want to apply toward these goals yet. We'll determine the right amount in *Week 7 - My First Budget*.

If you are ready to work on those large recurring headache bills, you'll need to figure out the right amount to set aside for them each month. In case you don't remember, these are bills that come due every once in a while, such as car insurance and taxes. When those large bills come due, the amount is so large that either those bills or other smaller bills don't get paid on time. They really are a headache! There are three variables that you should consider in your calculations to determine the right amount to set aside in your budget:

- Target Date
- Target Amount
- Minimum Monthly Amount

If you know any two of the above variables, you can calculate the remaining one. Target Date is the date the bill is going to come due, probably several months down the road. Target Amount is the total amount of the upcoming bill. Minimum Monthly Amount is the amount you will need to set aside each month so that when the time comes to pay the bill, you will have accumulated enough money to pay the bill. Since you know when large recurring bills come due and how much they will cost you, you just need to set aside the right amount of money each month. The formula to calculate what that amount should be is pretty simple:

Step 1: Count the number of months left until the bill comes due, including the current month.

Step 2: Divide target amount by number of months left before bill comes due.

As an example, let's say your car insurance payment of $300 is coming due in three months. $300 ÷ 3 = $100. $100 is the amount you should set aside each month and allow to accumulate so that when the bill comes due, the money to pay for it has already been saved. Write down in your list of bills an entry for each of those large recurring headaches you have.

You can use a similar technique when trying to save enough money to build up your cash stash. For this goal, you know you want $250, and you might be planning to set aside $50 a month. To calculate what your target date would be, you simply divide $250 by $50, which is five months. In short, it will take you five months to build up your cash stash if you set aside only $50 per month. When you're ready, do the same for your "grand" reserves. If you do not have your cash stash or "grand" reserves yet, write them down in your list of bills to be paid. These are bills you will be paying to yourself.

If you are behind on a particular bill, you need to write in your list of bills one entry for the normal monthly bill and another entry for the amount you are behind. As we build our budget in the next week, we'll be able to determine how far caught up we can get on those bills.

How about those much-needed repairs? You might be thinking you have a list of bills so long that you can't possibly be able to focus on those repairs. This may be true for now, but at least write them down as a bill we need to consider for the month. Having all those bills in front of you helps you be a little more frugal, reminding you that you need to take care of some other things before buying that new larger flat screen Super HD TV.

Do not be discouraged by the large list of bills you have staring you in the face. When I first got married, my wife and I had a combined couple dozen charge cards and loans to work our way through. The pain of working through all of those bills is one of the reasons I developed this budgeting process to begin with.

THE MONKEY TRAP

In some parts of the world such as Africa, Asia, and South America, the natives will set a simple trap to capture monkeys. They will bore a small hole either in the side of an old termite mound or in a large empty gourd and fill the empty vessel halfway with sand. They will then throw some food or a shiny object that the monkey finds irresistible into the hole. The monkey easily pushes its hand through the small hole and grabs the object of interest, but when it tries to pull its hand out, it cannot because its fist is now too big to fit back through the hole while it clutches the object. The monkey panics, screams, and yanks at its arm in a futile attempt to free itself. If only the monkey knew that all it had to do was let go of the shiny prize that so easily captivated its attention. Instead, it is driven by its selfish desire to not lose its newfound treasure and is willing to give up its freedom in order to keep the object in its hand.

You've put your list of bills together. What shiny object do you have in your hand that you aren't willing to do without? Are you trapped by the desire to keep hold of your possessions and desires at the cost of your freedom? When you owe someone something, you have guaranteed a portion of your future to be dedicated to that person in order to pay him or her back. You essentially become a servant; you are not free to do as you choose, you are trapped. You have to work to earn enough money not only to make a living but also to pay them back. Sometimes, the best solution is to let it go. Was the possession you are holding onto now a universal necessity ten, twenty, or thirty years ago? If people didn't need it then, why is it a necessity now? Are you going to let this selfish desire get in the way of achieving your goals and dreams?

What is this thing you hold so tightly, anyway? For some, it could be deluxe cable TV. What if you had basic cable, or even no cable? Would the world come to an abrupt end? I'm sure some would argue that it would. What about the car you are driving? Is your car payment more than your house payment? That might be a sign you need to let it go. Before you write all those bills down in your budget, ask yourself what it would be like not to have that bill, not dealing with the pressures of keeping that possession. Do you have control of it, or does it control you? What about some of those bad habits? Those cigarettes can get quite expensive. I've never been a smoker, but both my parents were chain smokers, so I understand it's not an easily broken habit. You may need some professional counseling to free yourself from the bonds of the addiction that has captivated you, whether that is a material possession or a bad habit. Compare the cost of these things against your financial goals. How far could you get with your goals if you weren't trapped by such a high car payment, along with the requisite high insurance, high taxes, and high repair bills? Maybe it's time to sell and get something more reasonable for a person in your financial position.

You may be in a worse situation if your spouse is the one holding onto the shiny object. It could be difficult to reason with him or her. Your wife may argue that it's just a small bill, or your husband may say that when you are willing to give up your shiny object, he might be willing to give up his. It's a tough situation to be in.

LIQUIDATION

Just as we did in *Week 5 - My Income*, I now want you to reconsider those things you still owe money on and whether or not they can be sold to pay off that debt. This serves two purposes: you get some extra income from the sale, and you reduce your monthly expenses. That's the best of both worlds, which is why you should seriously consider putting those things up for sale, if for no other reason than to free yourself of some of that debt. The price of freedom from debt may be less than you think.

A TIME TO REFLECT

In order to deal with this week's material, you will have to make some of the hardest decisions you'll make in a long time. However, don't do anything rash until you are fully armed with a completed budget so you know what you can and can't do. The hard part is done. Before moving to next week, take a moment to reflect on how far you have already come. You're doing great. Now it's time to open your eyes to the world of possibilities!

WEEK 6 – QUESTIONS & DISCUSSION
(You may copy this page as needed)

1. Name some "shiny objects" that you could possibly liquidate. What lifestyle changes would have to occur and how much would you save?

    _____
    _____
    _____

2. You've got a vacation you want to take in 5 months. You need $3,000 to pay for the condo and expenses. How much money do you need to set aside each much to pay for your vacation?

    _____

3. Name 2 ways you can reduce expenses.

    _____
    _____

4. PREPARE! Write down each expense you have on a separate piece of paper, along with the minimum payment amount and date the bill must be paid.

5. Review your list of expenses with your spouse and add to it anything you forgot to include. What was their reaction when they first saw the "list"?

    _____
    _____
    _____

6. TRUE or FALSE
    Your list of expenses should not contain any financial goals until all bills are caught up and paid on time.

WEEK 7 – MY FIRST BUDGET

INTRODUCING ONLINE BUDGETING

Now it's time to put the puzzle together and see what kind of financial picture you have drawn for yourself. You've considered your motives and goals, and you've balanced your checkbook. You've looked at all your sources of income and written them down, and you've taken inventory of all your bills and debt and written them down as well. Now comes the fun part: putting all of this together and creating your budget. It really is exciting to watch people do this for the first time as their eyes begin to open to the world of possibilities and hope.

Time is precious to us all. As I mentioned earlier, the ultimate purpose of *Budget Ninjas* is <u>not</u> to get you focused on your finances, but to get you in a position where you don't have to be. I want to make budgeting as easy as possible for you. If you are spending hours and hours each month trying to keep track of all the details through your spreadsheet or envelope system, you may be working hard than you need to be. I typically spend about 10 to 15 minutes each week on my budget. After you have gone through the process a few times, that's about the amount of time you'll need as well. I want you spending your time chasing your dreams and making an impact on those around you.

That's why I set out to develop an online budgeting system based on the concepts taught in this book. You need a system that takes the drudgery out of budgeting and makes it fun. You need a system that will quickly answer questions such as "Where did all my money go?" or "How can I afford to buy this new car?" You need a system that will help you step by step as you work to achieve your goals and fulfill your dreams. We'll use our free online **Budgeting Service** at www.budgetsteward.com. If you are working with a financial coach, they will sit with you as you get started on your first budget to make getting started simple and easy.

The following material is presented step-by-step so you can follow along on your own computer. At this time, you should be sitting at your computer and follow along the step by step instructions presented. We recommend using Chrome, Microsoft's Internet Explorer (Windows 7) or Microsoft Edge (Windows 10) browsers for optimal experience.

BUDGET NINJAS NAVIGATION

Navigate to our *Home* page at www.budgetsteward.com. Our home page provides information about our free services, links to the latest news and events, and other information of interest. The navigation bar at the top has all the major sections of our website listed, and it can be found on all of our pages.

The *Login* page provides access to your budgets. You must first register for your free account before you can login.

The *Show Me* page contains information about our free services (Budgeting and Projects) as well as optional services, such as Connections.

The *Calculators* page contains several free financial calculators that will assist you with your budget, such as the Accelerated Debt Payoff calculator, and the Mortgage Refinance calculator. We've already described many of those for you.

The *News* page contains a variety of helpful topics for saving money, eliminating debt, as well as news describing the latest features available in our system. You will also find links to prior newsletters and links to our Budget Buddy comic series, and Ninja Nuggets tips of the day.

The *Register* page allows you to establish a free account with Budget Ninjas. No credit card or personal information is required, other than a valid email address so you can recover your password should you ever forget it.

Browse around the web site to become familiar where everything is located. Once you are done, click the *Home* button or the icon at the top of the page.

REGISTERING

 Register for your free account by clicking the *Register* link. Registration does not require a credit card or any personal information other than a valid email address. The registration screen is shown in Figure 7-1.

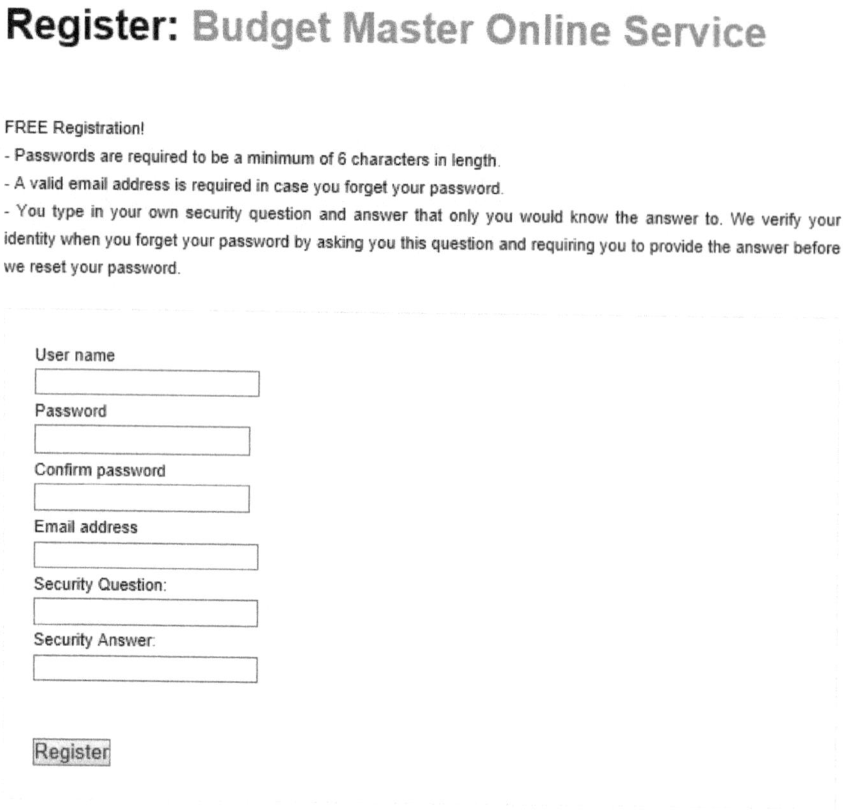

Register: Budget Master Online Service

FREE Registration!
- Passwords are required to be a minimum of 6 characters in length.
- A valid email address is required in case you forget your password.
- You type in your own security question and answer that only you would know the answer to. We verify your identity when you forget your password by asking you this question and requiring you to provide the answer before we reset your password.

User name
[   ]

Password
[   ]

Confirm password
[   ]

Email address
[   ]

Security Question:
[   ]

Security Answer:
[   ]

[Register]

FIGURE 7-1

Fill in the required fields. You can type in whatever you want for your security question and answer. If you should ever forget your password, we'll ask you this security question, and if you answer correctly, we'll email you a temporary password that you can use to log back in (which is a good reason to use a valid email address so we can use it to send you important information such as this).

After you successfully register, you are taken to the *Connect* tab. You also now have a few other options in the navigation bar – *Budget* and *Logoff*. *Connect* allows you to review options for your account, such as changing your contact information, email address, and contact preferences, as well as manage your connections to banks, budgets, and projects. The *Logoff* button ends your current session.

At this time, let's log off the system to insure you can log back in with the password you established. Press the *Logoff* button in the navigation bar now.

LOGIN

 Press the *Login* button to get back into the Budget Ninjas system so you can begin work on your budgets. The *Login* page is displayed in figure 7-2.

Login: Budget Master Online Service

Please login to access your budget and review your settings...forgot your password? Click Here

User name

Password

☐ Remember me?

[Log in]

FIGURE 7-2

Enter your user id and password and click the *Log in* button. Check the "Remember me?" box if you want the system to remember who you are so you do not have to log back in all the time. The "Remember me" feature is a great time saver, but please do not use it when accessing the system from a public computer. If you forget to log off, others could access your private information if they discover the link in the browser's history.

If you forget your password, click the link below the "forgot your password?" question. You will be asked for your user name and then we'll ask you the security question you entered when you registered. If you can successfully answer the security question, your password will be reset to a temporary password. We'll send it to the email address you provided when you registered. You will then be able to log back into the system. Go to *Show*

Me – Account Setting if you want to reset your password back to something easily remembered (see *Week 10 – Connect Features* for more details). If you are still unable to log in, call or email us at the contact information provided at the bottom of the page. We may ask several questions to confirm your identity before resetting the password for you.

After successful log in, the Home page is displayed again. Click the *Budget* link to access your budget. The following is displayed where you can start building your budget

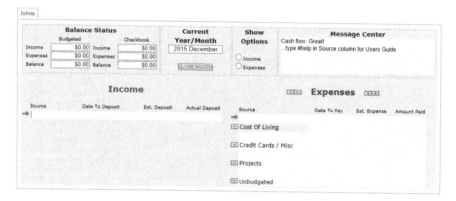

FIGURE 7-3

The *Budget* page provides you with all the details you need to successfully run a budget. Let's explore each of these areas to see what they are all about.

BALANCE STATUS

At the top left in the *Balance Status* area, you'll see a couple of summaries. One shows you whether your budget is balanced, and the other shows you what your checkbook balance should be. The *Checkbook Balance Status* section tells you what has already happened in your budget this month; in other words, it shows how much income you have earned and deposited, how much you have spent, and what balance should now show in your checkbook. Unless you are broke or overdrawn, you should always have a positive balance left in your checkbook. If the summary shows a negative amount in your checkbook, that means you wrote a check you don't have funds for or possibly that you forgot to record a deposit! The *Budgeted Balance Status* section is different. Initially, it is a summary of the money you are expecting to earn and to pay out for the month. When you are putting your budget together for the first time each month, you want your expected income to be greater than your expected expenses, or, as some prefer, your expected income and expected expenses to be equal. That is the definition of a balanced budget, and we'll go through the process to show you how to get to that point. After you set your initial budget and start depositing money and paying bills, the *Budgeted Balance Status* summary reflects the current state of your budget, taking into consideration the money you have already deposited and still have to deposit, as well as the bills you have already paid and have yet to pay. As we work our way through the budget, you will learn how to check these sections so you know where you stand at all times of the month.

CURRENT YEAR / MONTH

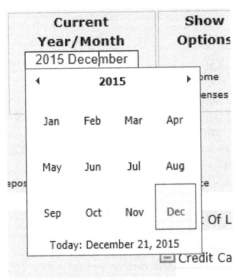

The *Current Year / Month* area is used to control the year and month you are working on. By default, it is set to the month and year for the current date.

The question you need to answer at this time is whether you want to start your budget for this month or the next month. If you are in the last week of the month, I would suggest setting up your budget for the following month, otherwise, leave the year and month as is. If you need to change the month, click on the current year and month shown to display a calendar that you can quickly scroll through to select the year and month desired (as shown).

The actual start date of your budget is based on your first income entry, which is normally the amount of money you currently have in the bank that can be used to pay for expenses. That means you can start your budget on any day of the month. If you want to start in the middle of the month, that's fine. You can then finish off the month, putting yourself in better position to start next month's budget. You might also want to consider starting on the day you get paid. That's helpful because it gives you money in the bank to work with if you don't have any already, and it helps you avoid the cash flow problems described later.

We keep a history of all your monthly budgets for you. I have sometimes had to go back several months to see what I paid for a bill that comes around only once a year so I could make sure I put the right amount in the current budget. It's also good to review your budget history to see how well you are progressing on your goals from one month to the next. In addition, I can look at my budget history to see how my power bill and water bill fluctuate at different times of the year, or I can go back and look at the winter months to see how much I had to pay for gas and electricity so I can know about what to expect for next winter.

Change the current year / month at any time to navigate to prior monthly budgets. When you are finished reviewing, change the year and month back to the current year and month to continue working on your latest budget. You can even move forward to the future if you want to pre-budget some upcoming expenses so you don't forget. This function might come in handy for anniversaries, birthdays, and other special occasions.

SHOW OPTIONS

If you noticed between the *Current Year/Month* and the *Message Center*, there is a *Show Options* section. These options come in use as you are entering income and expense entries, so we will cover those in more detail later as we begin to work those areas.

MESSAGE CENTER

The *Message Center* serves two purposes. The main purpose is to analyze your budget, check for potential problems, and give you a status update on how everything looks. The top row of the *Message Center* is reserved to inform you of the current state of your budget. If all is well, you will see the following comment: "Cash flow: Great!" What exactly are we checking for to determine if your budget is in great shape? Basically, we check to see if you are, or are going to be, running out of money. We also check if things are a little too tight for comfort, or if you have some outstanding updates you need to do. We do this every time you make a change to your budget. We want you "in the know" all the time, so we'll tell you when the problem starts, how much you are off, and if there is anything obvious you can do to correct the problem. Some messages, like the one shown in Figure 7-4, indicate potential serious issues you need to review immediately.

> **Message Center**
> Cash flow: NEGATIVE CHECKBOOK BALANCE! (#showmd)
> On 05-12, you were 83.44 short paying the Power Bill
> bill based on checkbook balance. Double check your entries!
> Fill in actual deposit for the 1 income entries past due.
> Budget: John (enter #hidemd to hide message details)

FIGURE 7-4

We try to give you as much detail as possible to help you resolve your issue. We will also list the name of the budget with the issue in case there are multiple budgets linked together (an advanced feature). In the example above, the problem was that John had forgotten to record his actual deposit on the income entry. The system saw that and figured it might be part of the problem. If you are facing multiple issues, we will deliver the most important messages to you first. As you correct each issue, we'll show you the next one in line.

The other purpose of the *Message Center* is to inform you of actions that have occurred as you make additions and changes to your budget, such as the following:

> **Message Center**
> Cash flow: Things are pretty tight (#showmd)
> ...expense entry added - Groceries
> ...expense entry updated - Power Bill
> ...income entry updated - In bank
> ...expense entry updated - Cable

We will show you the last four actions you performed that impacted your budget.

BUDGET MASTER COMMANDS

Did you notice the keyword "#showmd" in the *Message Center* comments? These keywords are part of the Budget Master Command Language you will become familiar with as you gain experience using the Budget Master Online Service.

In the Income and Expense data grids, the top row is reserved to allow you to make quick income or expense entries. We also look in the source column on that top row for any commands you want to execute. All commands start with "#" which is the hashtag symbol. If you want to see a current list of available commands, type in "#help" as shown here to display 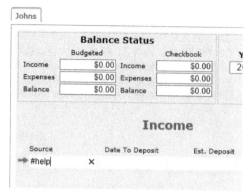 the Budget Master Users Guide. Look for the Budget Master Command Language entry at the bottom of the guide to display all of the commands at your disposal and what they can do for you to make your budgeting life easier.

At this time, enter #help in the source column as shown above, and then click the arrow next to "How to use this help". Follow the instructions in the first section of help. Press the *Hide* button or enter #nohelp to remove the guide from the screen.

Most of the functions the commands perform are available through other menu options, but using commands is much quicker. Some commands are only useful under certain circumstances, such as when you have linked budgets. Other commands such as "#showmd" are not available through a menu option, so the only way to access that function is to issue the command.

INCOME DATA GRID

You've got two sides to the budget equation, the left side (*Income*), and the right side (*Expenses*). Let's look closer at these individual areas to see how we use them to create our balanced budget.

I would like to introduce you to our fictitious family, the Smiths. John and Jane Smith are working on their first budget, and we'll watch them as they put everything together. Both Mr. and Mrs. Smith work, and they have two school-age kids and a dog named Spot. They are your typical middle-income family trying to understand why each month seems to be a financial struggle.

The first thing that Mr. Smith did earlier was balance their checkbook. He knows the exact amount of money they have in the bank. The money in the bank can be spent on upcoming bills and expenses, so it is income that has already been realized. This is the first entry he'll make in the *Income* area of the budget, the amount of money "In Bank" (see Figure 7-5).

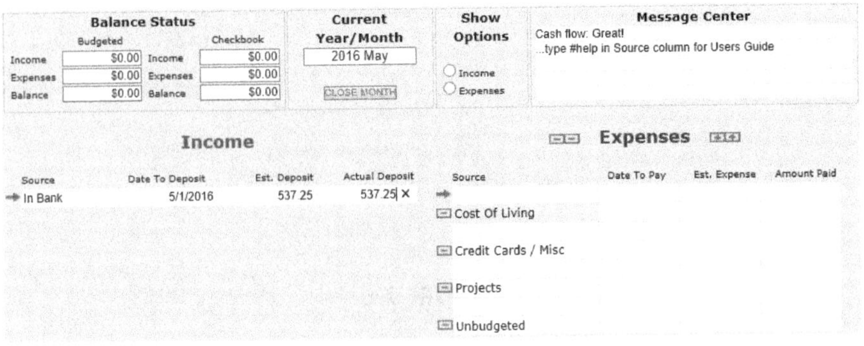

FIGURE 7-5

When making *Income* entries, you need to identify the *Source* of the income and the day you expect the money to be deposited into your checking account. In our "In Bank" entry, the *Date to Deposit* is the day you create your budget, since the money is already in the bank. The *Est. Deposit* amount is the actual amount you have in the bank, so you write the same number in that column and in the *Actual Deposit* column. Normally, you do not write anything in the *Actual Deposit* or *Amount Paid* columns until the money has been deposited or the bill has been paid.

Mr. & Mrs. Smith have $537.25 in their checking account, so you can see how he entered that amount in the *Income* section. After pressing the enter key, you can begin to see their financial story unfold in the *Balance Status* area as shown in Figure 7-6.

Balance Status			Current Year/Month	Show Options	Message Center
	Budgeted	Checkbook	2016 May		Cash flow: Great!
Income	$537.25	Income $537.25		○ Income	...income entry added - In bank
Expenses	$0.00	Expenses $0.00		○ Expenses	...type #help in Source column for Users Guide
Balance	$537.25	Balance $537.25	CLOSE MONTH		

Income ⊟⊞   **Expenses** ⊞⊟

Source	Date To Deposit	Est. Deposit	Actual Deposit	Source	Date To Pay	Est. Expense	Amount Paid
➡				➡			
➡ In bank	5/1/2016	537.25	537.25	⊟ Cost Of Living			
				⊟ Credit Cards / Misc			
				⊟ Projects			
				⊟ Unbudgeted			

FIGURE 7-6

In the *Budgeted Balance Status* section, they see they now have an expected income of $537.25, with no expected expenses, leaving them with a budget balance of $537.25. Of course, this will quickly change as they make more entries, but I want you to understand how that area works. In the *Checkbook Balance Status* section, they see they have actually deposited $537.25 in income, they have not paid any bills, and their checkbook balance is $537.25. The *Checkbook Balance Status* section shouldn't change anymore as you build your first budget, since you will not be depositing more income or paying any bills until after you have balanced your budget. Let's watch how this unfolds.

If you haven't already done so, balance your checkbook and enter your "In Bank" income entry on your budget. TIP! The "In Bank" entry is a special entry that the system looks for to help you move from one month to the next. When you close your budget for the month (explained later), we'll automatically set your "In Bank" entry for you for the following month based on the amount of money you have left in the month. So, even if you don't have any money in the bank to start with, go ahead and create an "In Bank" entry and enter 0's if you have to.

John gets paid every other week and Jane gets paid weekly. Both look carefully at the calendar and see on what days they will be paid next. They then enter a separate income entry for every time they are paid, and then press enter for each one on the "quick entry" top line. The amount they enter is the net, or bring-home income. They do not have any other sources of income right now, so here's what they end up with.

Balance Status			Current Year/Month	Show Options	Message Center
	Budgeted	Checkbook	2016 May		Cash flow: Great!
Income	$3,987.25 Income	$537.25		○ Income	...income entry updated - Jane
Expenses	$0.00 Expenses	$0.00		○ Expenses	...income entry updated - Jane
Balance	$3,987.25 Balance	$537.25	CLOSE MONTH		...income entry added - Jane
					...income entry added - John

Income				Expenses			
Source	Date To Deposit	Est. Deposit	Actual Deposit	Source	Date To Pay	Est. Expense	Amount Paid
⇒ I				⇒			
⇒ In bank	5/1/2016	537.25	537.25	⊟ Cost Of Living			
⇒ Jane	5/1/2016	250.00	0.00				
⇒ Jane	5/9/2016	250.00	0.00	⊟ Credit Cards / Misc			
⇒ John	5/10/2016	1100.00	0.00				
⇒ Jane	5/16/2016	250.00	0.00	⊟ Projects			
⇒ Jane	5/23/2016	250.00	0.00				
⇒ John	5/24/2016	1100.00	0.00	⊟ Unbudgeted			
⇒ Jane	5/30/2016	250.00	0.00				

FIGURE 7-7

The Smiths now have an estimated $3987.25 to work with for the month to pay their bills. This total comes from adding up everything in the *Est. Deposit* column. Notice that the only entry they have in the *Actual Deposit* column is the money they have already deposited in the bank. Since they haven't received their paychecks yet, they won't use the *Actual Deposit* column again until they start working their budget (described later). If you make a mistake entering your income entries, you can simply type over the existing values and press enter. If you need to delete an entry, click the arrow beside the item and choose the delete option.

The Smiths have their paychecks automatically deposited for them by their company, and they know on what dates those amounts will be deposited. If you are paid in cash, keep in mind that it may be the next day before you are able to go to the bank and make your deposit. I have been burnt a few times in the past by thinking I was going straight to the bank to make my deposit, only to find that the bank was closed for a holiday. You can't write checks or use your debit card for money that hasn't been deposited, so it is important that you try to be as accurate as you can when you write down the date the money will be deposited. This is the date when the bank recognizes the new money in your account as available funds to be used to pay bills. Some banks have made improvements in this area by providing real-time scans on teller machines for checks to be deposited and by giving customers same day credit. You don't even have to enter the amount of your deposit; the scanner will read it for you from the check. Some banks even let you scan your check with your smart phone, making your deposit from home or anywhere else! Technology really is great when it works.

Most of us know exactly how much we will be paid, so we are pretty confident that the amount we write in the *Est. Deposit* column is accurate.

However, some of you may work off of commissions or have a job where your hours fluctuate, causing your bring-home pay to fluctuate from paycheck to paycheck. You may not have the same level of confidence in the amount you are going to deposit as others do. If this describes you, then the basic rule of thumb is to write down an average of what you made in the prior three months (or similar months if the business you are in is seasonal), while at the same time considering your upcoming work opportunities. If you are still not sure what to estimate, then write in what you think you might make and lean more to the conservative side in case you don't do as well as you had hoped. Again, leave the *Actual Deposit* column blank at this time.

Now you need to consider other sources of income that you may earn during the month. Do you have an interest-bearing checking account? If so, write in the estimated interest to be earned, even if it is just a small amount. Expecting a bonus? Write it in! How about those wonderful income tax refunds? The more you can write down, the better off you'll be. The total of all your income will be used as a guide to determine how much you can safely spend for the month.

Notice that the entries the Smiths have made are automatically ordered by the *Date to Deposit* column. This helps you quickly see what's next to be deposited and when that deposit will take place.

Go ahead and enter all your income entries for the rest of the month. If you have written down your sources of income for the exercise in the previous week, check these sources off to make sure you don't forget anything. Review the *Balance Status* area. The *Budgeted Balance Status* section shows the amount of money you have to work with for the rest of the month. The *Checkbook Balance Status* section shows the amount of money you currently have in the bank. If these numbers do not look right to you, review your income entries and verify the amounts entered.

The alternative way to add an income entry is to click the arrow button on the left side of the quick entry line. The detail income entry panel is displayed as shown in Figure 7-8.

Balance Status				Current Year/Month	Show Options	Message Center
	Budgeted		Checkbook	2016 May		Cash flow: Great!
Income	$3,987.25	Income	$537.25		○ Income	...type #help in Source column for Users Guide
Expenses	$0.00	Expenses	$0.00		○ Expenses	
Balance	$3,987.25	Balance	$537.25	CLOSE MONTH		

Income

Source	Date To Deposit	Est. Deposit	Actual Deposit
⇥			
⇥ In bank	5/1/2016	537.25	537.25
⇥ Jane	5/1/2016	250.00	0.00
⇥ Jane	5/9/2016	250.00	0.00
⇥ John	5/10/2016	1100.00	0.00
⇥ Jane	5/16/2016	250.00	0.00
⇥ Jane	5/23/2016	250.00	0.00
⇥ John	5/24/2016	1100.00	0.00
⇥ Jane	5/30/2016	250.00	0.00

Details

Source
Date To Deposit
Est. Deposit
Actual Deposit

Budget: Johns ▾

Tags (optional):

(example: #mypaycheck, #bonus)

Back   Add

FIGURE 7-8

In addition to the four columns from the quick entry line, you have access to some additional fields. If your budget is linked to another, and you have full control rights to that other budget, you can choose to make this income entry belong to the other budget instead.

Tagging your entries is an optional feature that will allow you to group common income entries together. Any given income entry can have multiple tags; therefore, tags should start with the hashtag symbol so the system can easily recognize where one tag begins and another one ends. Once you tag an item, the system remembers the tag from one month to the next, so you only need to enter it once for an income or expense entry that recurs every month.

You can also press the arrow button beside an existing income entry to change the values previously entered. This is helpful when you want to go back and tag previous income entries. You also have the option to delete an entry on the income detail panel.

If all you need to do is update one of the four columns shown on the main income data grid, you can make the change right there on multiple rows at the same time. When you press enter, all rows are updated immediately. This feature makes it extraordinarily easy to keep your budget updated with actual information as the month progresses.

EXPENSE DATA GRID

The *Expenses* area is almost identical to the *Income* area, and the only changes are slight adjustments to the headings. Here, you have your *Source* of expense, the *Date to Pay* the expense, the *Est. Expense* amount, and *Amount Paid* columns.

⊡⊡ **Expenses** ⊡⊞			
Source	Date To Pay	Est. Expense	Amount Paid
➡			
⊟ Cost Of Living			
⊟ Credit Cards / Misc			
⊟ Projects			
⊟ Unbudgeted			

Before you start entering all of your individual bills, a discussion of the various categories of bills is in order as you will separate your bills into these groups. You will realize how important this categorization is as you tackle the problems of balancing the budget, keeping the cash flowing, and paying off debt. Each budget should be comprised of the following categories:

Cost of Living: These are the bills you face every month that will never go away or cannot be paid off in a reasonable amount of time. This includes house payments or rent, car payments, insurance and taxes, utilities, groceries, etc. They are the must-pay-to-live bills.

Credit Cards / Misc: These are the bills that can be paid off in a reasonable amount of time or are one-time expenses that you know you will incur during the month and would like to include in your budget. Examples include charge cards, consumer loans, and student loans. Other one-time expenses might be clothing, birthday presents, and holiday expenses.

Projects: Projects is the area where you will make entries for your financial goals, like saving for your cash stash, or grand reserves. Project expenses can either be entered directly by you, or by the system if you use the Project tracking tool (explained later). Those expenses coming from the Project tracking tool are automatically placed here so you can see the impact those project expenses have on your budget.

UNBUDGETED: This is the category that gets most people in trouble. When you first create your budget for a given month, this category is empty. As you work your budget, though, any bills you pay with your checking account that were not previously budgeted go here. Hopefully, this section will remain empty.

Cost of Living

Now that you understand the categories of the *Expenses* area, let's start off by entering expenses for our "Cost of Living" category. There are three ways you can add expense entries: quick entry, detail entry and using the template.

Quick entry is very easy. Simply type the information desired on the top line of the Expense data grid, like this:

	Expenses		
Source	Date To Pay	Est. Expense	Amount Paid
➡ Groceries 1	5/3/2016	130.00	0.00
▣ Cost Of Living			
▣ Credit Cards / Misc			
▣ Projects			
▣ Unbudgeted			

Press enter and your expense entry is added. You will now see something similar to what is shown in Figure 7-9.

Balance Status				**Current Year/Month**	**Show Options**	**Message Center**
	Budgeted		Checkbook	2016 May		Cash flow: Great!
Income	$3,987.25	Income	$537.25		○ Income	...expense entry added - Groceries 1
Expenses	$130.00	Expenses	$0.00		○ Expenses	...type #help in Source column for Users Guide
Balance	$3,857.25	Balance	$537.25	CLOSE MONTH		

Income   **Expenses**

Source	Date To Deposit	Est. Deposit	Actual Deposit	Source	Date To Pay	Est. Expense	Amount Paid
➡				➡			
➡ In bank	5/1/2016	537.25	537.25	▣ Cost Of Living			
➡ Jane	5/1/2016	250.00	0.00	➡ Groceries 1	5/3/2016	130.00	0.00
➡ Jane	5/9/2016	250.00	0.00				
➡ John	5/10/2016	1100.00	0.00	▣ Credit Cards / Misc			
➡ Jane	5/16/2016	250.00	0.00				
➡ Jane	5/23/2016	250.00	0.00	▣ Projects			
➡ John	5/24/2016	1100.00	0.00				
➡ Jane	5/30/2016	250.00	0.00	▣ Unbudgeted			

FIGURE 7-9

Notice how the entry was automatically added to the "Cost of Living" category. The "Cost of Living" category is the default category to which new expense entries will be added until you change that default. You know it's the current default because the category heading is shaded in gray as shown in Figure 7-9. It is very easy to change the default category; all you have to do is click on the desired category heading. Once the chosen category is shaded in gray, you know it is the current default.

Another way to enter expenses is through the detail entry display. Click the arrow button on the left side of the quick entry line. The detail expense entry panel is displayed as shown in Figure 7-10.

Details

Source	
Date To Pay	
Est. Expense	
Actual Paid	

Category: Cost Of Living ⌄

Budget: Johns ⌄

Tags (optional):

(example: #utilities, #school)

[Back] [Add]

FIGURE 7-10

In addition to the four columns from the quick entry line, you have access to some additional fields. You can select the category the expense should fall under. If your budget is linked to another, and you have full control rights to that other budget, you can choose to make this expense entry belong to the other budget instead.

Tagging your entries is an optional feature that will allow you to group common expense entries together. Any given expense entry can have multiple tags; therefore, tags should start with the hashtag symbol so the system can easily recognize where one tag begins and another one ends. Once you tag an item, the system remembers the tag from one month to the next, so you only need to enter it once for an income or expense entry that recurs every month. You can also press the arrow button beside an existing expense entry to change the values previously entered. This is helpful when you want to go back and tag previous expense entries. You also have the option to delete an entry on the expense detail panel.

Options

Start with a template:

[Preview]

Default category to use when adding new entries:

[Cost Of Living ▾]

Outstanding & Completed Filters:

◉ Show both outstanding and completed expense entries (#ae)

○ Show only outstanding expense entries (#oe)

○ Show only completed expense entries (#ce)

[Back]

The third method you can use to enter expenses is through the expense template. Under "Show Options", click on Expense, and then click "Start with a template" Preview button. Pick the expense entries you want in your budget and then click Proceed (see Figure 7-11). The selected items are copied to your budget where you can adjust amounts and dates as needed.

Start With a Template

Use our Quick-Start template to quickly kick-start your budget to include common expense entries. Use the grid on the right to choose which expense items you want to include in your budget. Some expenses are listed multiple times for those expenses that are likely to occur on a weekly basis. Choose the expenses that make sense for you and how you spend your money. The dates will be set to the current month. After the process completes, you can adjust the dates and amounts as you see fit. Press "Proceed" when you are ready, or "Back" if you changed your mind.

[**Proceed**]

[Back]

Items Checked Are Copied

Source	Date To Pay	Est. Expense	Amount Paid
Cost Of Living			
☐ Giving - Building Fund	12/1/2015	1.00	0.00
☐ Giving - Charitable Organiza	12/1/2015	1.00	0.00
☐ Giving - Christmas Gifts	12/1/2015	1.00	0.00
☐ Housing - Mortgage - 1st	12/2/2015	1.00	0.00
☐ Housing - Mortgage - 2nd	12/2/2015	1.00	0.00
☐ Housing - Telephone	12/2/2015	1.00	0.00
☐ Housing - Bug Man	12/2/2015	1.00	0.00
☐ Housing - NIPSCO	12/2/2015	1.00	0.00
☐ Housing - Internet	12/2/2015	1.00	0.00
☐ Hosuing - REMC	12/2/2015	1.00	0.00
☐ Housing - Culligan	12/2/2015	1.00	0.00
☐ Housing - Homeowners Insu	12/2/2015	1.00	0.00
☐ Housing - Rent	12/2/2015	1.00	0.00

FIGURE 7-11

Review the list of expenses you wrote down from *Week 6 – My Bills*. Enter the ones you believe qualify as a Cost of Living expense, checking them off your list as you enter them in your budget. In the *Date to Pay* column, write in the date you expect this bill to be paid. In the *Est. Expense* column, enter the amount of the bill. If you do not know the exact amount, make an educated guess based on past history and your personal experience with that bill. Leave the *Amount Paid* column blank at this time. You will not be making entries here until you begin working your budget.

As much as possible and practical, you should have a separate entry for every "cost of living" transaction that will affect your checkbook. Let's look at the "cost of living" expenses that the Smiths have entered.

Balance Status				Current Year/Month	Show Options	Message Center
	Budgeted		Checkbook	2016 May		Cash flow: Things are pretty tight (#showmd)
Income	$3,987.25	Income	$537.25			...expense entry added - House payment
Expenses	$3,447.00	Expenses	$0.00		○ Income	...expense entry added - Gas card
Balance	$540.25	Balance	$537.25	CLOSE MONTH	○ Expenses	...expense entry added - Cable
						...expense entry added - Cell phone

Income

Source	Date To Deposit	Est. Deposit	Actual Deposit
➡			
➡ In bank	5/1/2016	537.25	537.25
➡ Jane	5/1/2016	250.00	0.00
➡ Jane	5/9/2016	250.00	0.00
➡ John	5/10/2016	1100.00	0.00
➡ Jane	5/16/2016	250.00	0.00
➡ Jane	5/23/2016	250.00	0.00
➡ John	5/24/2016	1100.00	0.00
➡ Jane	5/30/2016	250.00	0.00

Expenses

Source	Date To Pay	Est. Expense	Amount Paid
➡			
⊟ Cost Of Living			
➡ Groceries 1	5/3/2016	130.00	0.00
➡ Weekly cash 1	5/3/2016	150.00	0.00
➡ Car payment	5/4/2016	437.00	0.00
➡ House phone	5/5/2016	45.00	0.00
➡ Groceries 2	5/10/2016	130.00	0.00
➡ Weekly cash 2	5/10/2016	150.00	0.00
➡ Power bill	5/12/2016	165.00	0.00
➡ Cell phone	5/13/2016	110.00	0.00
➡ Groceries 3	5/17/2016	130.00	0.00
➡ Weekly cash 3	5/17/2016	150.00	0.00
➡ Cable	5/22/2016	45.00	0.00
➡ Groceries 4	5/24/2016	130.00	0.00
➡ Weekly cash 4	5/24/2016	150.00	0.00
➡ Gas card	5/25/2016	320.00	0.00
➡ Groceries 5	5/31/2016	130.00	0.00
➡ Weekly cash 5	5/31/2016	150.00	0.00
➡ House payment	5/31/2016	925.00	0.00
⊟ Credit Cards / Misc			
⊟ Projects			
⊟ Unbudgeted			

FIGURE 7-12

Notice all of the cost of living expenses the Smiths have entered already in Figure 7-12. Jane likes to go grocery shopping once a week, so we see a separate entry for each week of the month. Instead of making one entry for groceries for the entire month, they need five entries, one for each week they will be buying groceries. As they shop each week, they record the amount of money they spend. If you follow the Smiths' example, you will have a better idea of how closely you are keeping to your budget. Some folks don't like to shop in bulk at all. Instead, they go to the grocery store each day and pick up what they need. That's perfectly fine, but it does raise the number of transactions you have to deal with in your budget. If you go to the store several times a week, continue to limit your budget entry for groceries to once a week. Put a little note or something in the checkbook that lets you know this entry is part of your groceries expense for the week. You might write 'G1" next to the entry, meaning this amount is part of groceries expense for Week 1. At the end of the week, add up all your "G1" entries to see what your total expense was for groceries that week, and then enter the amount in your budget. Of course, we're not ready to enter actual amounts just yet.

The Smiths also like to withdraw some cash each week to be used for eating out, going to movies, and other miscellaneous expenses because it is more convenient to use cash and they don't have to keep up with so many details in their checking account. It's a smart move on their part to limit the details they have to work with on their budget, but it does conceal where some of their money is being spent. In the budget, they see "Weekly Cash," but how was that money actually spent? It's not necessary for you to keep track of every penny, but keep in mind that some of your expenses will be hidden if you choose to combine expenses in this way. Know what items you like to spend cash on, and as long as you are consistent, you should be able to easily explain where the money went if the question arises.

I dislike months like the one shown in Figure 7-12 because there are five weeks in the month, but since I only get paid every other week, I am only paid for four. John has the same problem; as you can see, he only receives two bi-weekly paychecks. Jane is fine, though, because she gets paid weekly and is expecting five paychecks. Months like these are usually more expensive because you have extra weekly bills like groceries, gas, and weekly cash that you need to plan for. That extra week of bills can add up to a lot of money and cause a lot of pain and heartache during the month as you try to budget for it. Just be aware of the situation so you can explain why you had so much more money left over last month than this month.

As it stands now, if the Smiths were finished entering their expenses, they would be in pretty good shape. They have a total expected income of $3987.25 for the month and total expected expenses of only $3447.00, leaving them with $540.25 left over that they can apply toward expenses in one of the other categories.

Notice that the Smiths have used nice round numbers for their projected expenses. You may already have the bill in hand with the exact amount to the penny, but if you want to simplify your work, you can pay your bills in whole numbers as well. Let's say you receive a power bill for $49.37. When you write the check, make it out for an even $50. The power company will give you a $.63 credit on your next bill, and you will have greatly simplified your check-balancing and budget-balancing process.

Credit Cards / Misc

Let's move on now to the "Credit Cards/Misc" category. Make it the default category by clicking on the category heading and it is shown shaded in gray. The other way you can change default category is through the Expense options.

Anything you add to the quick entry line will now be added to the "Credit Cards/Misc." category. Again, review the list of expenses you wrote down from *Week 6 – My Bills.* Enter the ones you believe qualify as a *Credit Cards / Misc* expense, checking them off your list as you enter them in your budget. Notice that as you do, the *Balance Status* section is updated for you, and the *Message Center* keeps you informed of potential problems that may be present. Don't worry about any of the messages at this time as we will work on correcting budget issues in Week 8.

Enter all your various charge cards, consumer loans, student loans, and any one-time expenses that you expect to pay during the month. In the *Date to Pay* column, enter the date by which these bills need to be paid. When you enter your dates on the data grid, you can either click on the date you want in the calendar or type in the month and day as mm/dd. The system knows which year it is and will fill in the rest for you. If you mistype a date, the system will default to the current date. In the *Est. Expense* column, for charge cards and loans, first write in the minimum monthly payment required by the company. You will come back later and adjust these when you work on balancing your budget in the next week, especially if you are at the point in your pursuit of financial goals where you can tackle debt. For one-time expenses, go ahead and write in the estimated amount of that expense. Leave the *Amount Paid* column blank at this time. You will not be making entries in this column until you begin working your budget next week.

If you need to update one of the four columns shown on the main expense data grid, you can make the change right there in multiple rows at the same time. Just as in the main income data grid, when you press enter, all rows are updated immediately. Thus, you may easily keep your budget updated with actual information as the month progresses.

Notice that on the charge cards and loans in Figure 7 – 13, the Smiths wrote in the total balance beside the description in the *Source* column. This information will come in handy later as you try to decide which bills to tackle first for debt elimination.

BUDGET NINJAS

Balance Status				Current Year/Month	Show Options	Message Center
	Budgeted		Checkbook	2016 May		Cash flow: Things are pretty tight (#showmd)
Income	$3,987.25	Income	$537.25			...expense entry added - Charge 2 ($4500)
Expenses	$3,537.00	Expenses	$0.00	CLOSE MONTH	○ Income	...expense entry added - Charge 1 ($755)
Balance	$450.25	Balance	$537.25		○ Expenses	...expense entry added - Furniture ($2350)
						...type #help in Source column for Users Guide

Income

Source	Date To Deposit	Est. Deposit	Actual Deposit
In bank	5/1/2016	537.25	537.25
Jane	5/1/2016	250.00	0.00
Jane	5/9/2016	250.00	0.00
John	5/10/2016	1100.00	0.00
Jane	5/16/2016	250.00	0.00
Jane	5/23/2016	250.00	0.00
John	5/24/2016	1100.00	0.00
Jane	5/30/2016	250.00	0.00

Expenses

Source	Date To Pay	Est. Expense	Amount Paid
Cost Of Living			
Groceries 1	5/3/2016	130.00	0.00
Weekly cash 1	5/3/2016	150.00	0.00
Car payment	5/4/2016	437.00	0.00
House phone	5/5/2016	45.00	0.00
Groceries 2	5/10/2016	130.00	0.00
Weekly cash 2	5/10/2016	150.00	0.00
Power bill	5/12/2016	165.00	0.00
Cell phone	5/13/2016	110.00	0.00
Groceries 3	5/17/2016	130.00	0.00
Weekly cash 3	5/17/2016	150.00	0.00
Cable	5/22/2016	45.00	0.00
Groceries 4	5/24/2016	130.00	0.00
Weekly cash 4	5/24/2016	150.00	0.00
Gas card	5/25/2016	320.00	0.00
Groceries 5	5/31/2016	130.00	0.00
Weekly cash 5	5/31/2016	150.00	0.00
House payment	5/31/2016	925.00	0.00
Credit Cards / Misc			
Furniture ($2350)	5/7/2016	25.00	0.00
Charge 1 ($755)	5/15/2016	15.00	0.00
Charge 2 ($4500)	5/31/2016	50.00	0.00
Projects			
Unbudgeted			

FIGURE 7-13

As it stands now, the Smiths show total Budgeted Expenses of $3537.00 and now have a budget balance of $450.25. That's great news for them because it means they can now go back to their list of expenses and consider what projects they would like to add to their budget. Speaking of which, how are you doing on your budget? Take one last look at your list of expenses. You should have them all checked off except for those expenses related to projects and other financial goals.

Next week, we'll finish our initial budget entries for Projects as part of budget balancing process. In the meantime, let's look at some additional navigational tips that will enhance your budgeting experience.

NAVIGATIONAL TIPS

You may end up with more expenses than you can see on the screen without having to scroll down the page. If you want to temporarily hide all the expenses in one of the categories, just press the collapse button to the

Cost Of Living
Groceries 1
Weekly cash 1

left of the category name (looks like a "minus" sign inside a box). Here's what the Smith's saw when they pressed the collapse button beside the "Cost of Living" category.

Balance Status			Current Year/Month	Show Options	Message Center
Budgeted		Checkbook	2016 May		Cash flow: Things are pretty tight (#showmd)
Income	$3,987.25	Income $537.25		○ Income	...type #help in Source column for Users Guide
Expenses	$3,537.00	Expenses $0.00		○ Expenses	
Balance	$450.25	Balance $537.25	CLOSE MONTH		

Income   ⊟⊟ **Expenses** ⊞⊞

Source	Date To Deposit	Est. Deposit	Actual Deposit		Source	Date To Pay	Est. Expense	Amount Paid
⇒					⇒|			
⇒ In bank	5/1/2016	537.25	537.25		⊞ Cost Of Living			
⇒ Jane	5/1/2016	250.00	0.00					
⇒ Jane	5/9/2016	250.00	0.00		⊟ Credit Cards / Misc			
⇒ John	5/10/2016	1100.00	0.00		⇒ Furniture ($2350)	5/7/2016	25.00	0.00
⇒ Jane	5/16/2016	250.00	0.00		⇒ Charge 1 ($755)	5/15/2016	15.00	0.00
⇒ Jane	5/23/2016	250.00	0.00		⇒ Charge 2 ($4500)	5/31/2016	50.00	0.00
⇒ John	5/24/2016	1100.00	0.00					
⇒ Jane	5/30/2016	250.00	0.00		⊟ Projects			
					⊟ Unbudgeted			

FIGURE 7-14

All of the "Cost of Living" expenses are hidden, allowing you to focus your attention on the category you are working on. An expand button (looks like a "plus" sign inside a box) now appears beside the "Cost of Living" category so you can show those entries whenever you want.

At the top of the expense panel, you will see two different buttons that surround the *Expenses* heading. The one on the left allows you to collapse all categories at once, while the one on the right allows you to expand all categories at once.

The following is a complete list of Budget Master Commands you can issue to accomplish the same thing:

#expall – Expand all expense categories
#expcol – Expand Cost Of Living expense category
#expccm – Expand Credit Cards / Miscellaneous expense category
#expp – Expand Projects expense category
#expu – Expend Unbudgeted expense category
#colall – Collapse all expense categories
#colcol – Collapse Cost Of Living expense category
#colccm – Collapse Credit Cards / Miscellaneous expense category
#colp – Collapse Projects expense category
#colu – Collapse Unbudgeted expense category

WEEK 7 – QUESTIONS & DISCUSSION
(You may copy this page as needed)

1. What is the first income entry you should make and why?

    _____

    _____

    _____

2. TRUE or FALSE.

    Your budgeted balance and checkbook balance should always match. If it doesn't, you are out of balance.

3. Name some common expenses you would include in the Cost of Living category.

    _____

    _____

    _____

4. Did you have any expenses that you could not determine what category they belonged in? List those here and discuss with the group.

    _____

    _____

    _____

5. Why would we initially enter only the minimum payments required for credit cards and other loans?

    _____

    _____

    _____

6. When first preparing your budget for the month, what is the only entry that should have an amount entered in the "Actual Deposit" or "Amount Paid" column?

    _____

WEEK 8 – FINISHING YOUR BUDGET

CASH FLOW

In week 7, you entered all of your normal income and expense entries. Take a look at the *Balance Status* and *Message Center* sections to see where you stand. You are now at the stage in your budget setup where you need to understand the possible cash flow issues and how to resolve each one so you can finish your initial budget. The basic principle of cash flow is that you want to make sure that at all times during the month, you always have enough money in the bank to cover your budgeted expenses. The system will alert you when this is not true. It is one thing to have a balanced budget (income greater than or equal to expenses), but you also need to make sure you have a positive cash flow. If most of your expenses are incurred near the beginning of the month and most of your income arrives at the end of the month, you are likely to run out of money in your checking account, and thus you won't be able to pay your bills on time. No budget is worth the paper it is written on if you cannot use it to pay your bills when they come due.

Look at the Cash Flow Worksheet that I manually prepared for the Smith's in Figure 8-1. You won't have to fill this out since the system does it for you, but I wanted to demonstrate how cash flow works. Think of it as a race. During the race, income should always stay ahead of expenses.

As of this Day of The Month	My Total Budgeted Income	My Total Budgeted Expenses
1	787.25	0.00
2	787.25	0.00
3	787.25	280.00
4	787.25	717.00
5	787.25	762.00
6	787.25	762.00
7	787.25	787.00
8	787.25	787.00
9	1037.25	787.00
10	2137.25	1067.00
11	2137.25	1067.00
12	2137.25	1232.00
13	2137.25	1342.00
14	2137.25	1342.00
15	2137.25	1357.00
16	2387.25	1357.00
17	2387.25	1637.00
18	2387.25	1637.00
19	2387.25	1637.00
20	2387.25	1637.00
21	2387.25	1637.00
22	2387.25	1682.00
23	2637.25	1682.00
24	3737.25	1962.00
25	3737.25	2282.00
26	3737.25	2282.00
27	3737.25	2282.00
28	3737.25	2282.00
29	3737.25	2282.00
30	3987.25	2282.00
31	3987.25	3537.25

FIGURE 8-1

The Smith family started off with cash on Day 1 because they have money already in bank on Day 1. Jane also got paid on Days 1 and 9, and John got paid on Day 10 and so on. On each day they got paid, they added the amount to be deposited to the previous total to get the total income received as of that day of the month. The Smith family has bills that come due on the 3rd, 4th, 5th, and so on.

As you can see, at no time during the month do the total expenses for any given day exceed total income for that same day; therefore, the Smiths have a positive cash flow. It is interesting to see that on Days 7 and 8, they are running very low on cash. It seems that if the income and bills come in as projected, they will only have about 25 cents left in their checking account on those days. With this knowledge in hand, they now know that they do not have a lot of extra money they can spend if a need arises. That's why it is so important to build your cash stash and "grand" reserves quickly. If you have already built them up, you can leave the "grand" reserves in your checking account, increasing the amount of money already in the bank on Day 1 so that cash flow problems like this do not become a real problem should something unexpected happen. If you do leave your reserves in your checking account, make sure you continue to list it as an expense to be paid at the end of the month. You'll never actually pay it, but you need the expense item there so you don't end up spending your reserves.

If you are in the unfortunate position where there are one or more days when total budgeted expenses exceed total budgeted income, the system will display the following message: "Cash flow: PROBLEMS LATER IN MONTH!".

> **Message Center**
>
> Cash flow: PROBLEMS LATER IN MONTH! (#showmd)
> On 05-12, you will be 94.75 short paying the Power bill
> bill. Please adjust accordingly to insure you can pay it.
> Budget: Johns (enter #hidemd to hide message details)

Use the "#showmd" (show message details) command to see exactly when the problem starts. This message only tells you about the first bill it encounters with a problem. Look at your budget balance to see how bad it really is, as you may likely have other bills beyond this date that may not be able to be paid as well.

You have two courses of action to correct this problem: increase income or decrease expenses. To decrease expenses, first look at the one-time expenses you have entered in the "Credit Cards/Misc." category. Seriously consider whether or not some of these items can be put off until a future month. Next, look at your various "Cost of Living" expenses and consider either eliminating or reducing some of these bills, if at all possible. You may need to turn in your cellular phone, cut out trips to a restaurant, or even cut the cable. After you have done your trimming, check your budget balance and see if your total budgeted expenses are now lower than your budgeted income. If not, then go to your Income Sheet and determine if there is any way to increase income. Could you put in some overtime? How about a garage sale? You've wanted to clean out that dusty attic for a while, and now would be the perfect time. If you can increase income, add or adjust income entries and then see if you now have more budgeted income than budgeted expenses. If you are still in the red, more drastic measures may be called for. You may need to trade in that luxury all-terrain vehicle for something that is a little more affordable, or you might want to consider getting another part-time job. You have to do something so that your total budgeted income exceeds or equals your total budgeted expenses. Do not proceed until this is done.

The next potential warning you will get from the system is the following

Message Center

Cash flow: Things are pretty tight (#showmd)
On 05-05, your checkbook balance is projected to be only
25.25. Watch your budget closely to stay on track.
Budget: Johns (enter #hidemd to hide message details)

message: "Cash flow: Things are pretty tight". If your projected checkbook balance at any time is $50 or less, you'll see this message. If we look back the cash flow worksheet I prepared for the Smith's back in Figure 8-1, you can see that on the 5th day, the difference between our projected income and expenses was indeed $25.25. The problem gets worse on day 7 where they only have a projected 25 cents left. This means you need to watch your budget very closely! If you have any significant unbudgeted expenses that you incur close to the beginning of the month, you could be jeopardizing your cash flow position. When this happens, you need to consider both where the money for this expense is going to come from and how this will affect your ability to pay future bills on time.

Pre-budgeting periodic expenses like car insurance can prevent cash flow problems if you keep the money you have accumulated in your checking account. This allows you to always start off the month with more money in the bank to last you until your next paycheck.

At this time, make sure your budget has been adjusted enough so you at least do not see the "PROBLEMS" cash flow message in the message center.

BALANCING YOUR BUDGET

PROJECTS

Now, let's pretend you are in the same situation as the Smiths. You have entered all your normal expenses, and you still have a little bit of money to play with (your budget balance is positive). Where does this money go? Hopefully, if all goes according to plan, you will still have this money available at the end of the month to apply to one or more of your financial goals.

FINANCIAL GOAL #1 – YOUR CASH STASH
FINANCIAL GOAL #2 – YOUR "GRAND" RESERVES
FINANCIAL GOAL #3 – LARGE RECURRING HEADACHES
FINANCIAL GOAL #4 – GETTING CAUGHT UP
FINANCIAL GOAL #5 – MUCH-NEEDED REPAIRS
FINANCIAL GOAL #6 – FREE MONEY
FINANCIAL GOAL #7 – SHORT-TERM SUCCESS
FINANCIAL GOAL #8 – WORKING RESERVES
FINANCIAL GOAL #9 – THE LONG HAUL

I recommend working these goals into your budget in the order listed above. The Smiths do not have a cash stash yet, so they are going to put $250 of the money they have left toward completing their first goal. They then plan to apply the remaining money toward the next financial goal, their "grand" reserves as shown in Figure 8-2.

Balance Status			Current Year/Month	Show Options	Message Center
Budgeted		Checkbook	2016 May		Cash flow: Things are pretty tight (#showmd)
Income	$3,987.25 Income	$537.25			...expense entry added - FG2 - Grand Reserves
Expenses	$3,987.25 Expenses	$0.00		○ Income	...expense entry added - FG1 - Cash Stash
Balance	$0.00 Balance	$537.25	CLOSE MONTH	○ Expenses	...type #help in Source column for Users Guide

Income

Source	Date To Deposit	Est. Deposit	Actual Deposit
⇒ In bank	5/1/2016	537.25	537.25
⇒ Jane	5/1/2016	250.00	0.00
⇒ Jane	5/9/2016	250.00	0.00
⇒ John	5/10/2016	1100.00	0.00
⇒ Jane	5/16/2016	250.00	0.00
⇒ Jane	5/23/2016	250.00	0.00
⇒ John	5/24/2016	1100.00	0.00
⇒ Jane	5/30/2016	250.00	

Expenses

Source	Date To Pay	Est. Expense	Amount Paid
⇒			
⊟ Cost Of Living			
⇒ Groceries 1	5/3/2016	130.00	0.00
⇒ Weekly cash 1	5/3/2016	150.00	0.00
⇒ Car payment	5/4/2016	437.00	0.00
⇒ House phone	5/5/2016	45.00	0.00
⇒ Groceries 2	5/10/2016	130.00	0.00
⇒ Weekly cash 2	5/10/2016	150.00	0.00
⇒ Power bill	5/12/2016	165.00	0.00
⇒ Cell phone	5/13/2016	110.00	0.00
⇒ Groceries 3	5/17/2016	130.00	0.00
⇒ Weekly cash 3	5/17/2016	150.00	0.00
⇒ Cable	5/22/2016	45.00	0.00
⇒ Groceries 4	5/24/2016	130.00	0.00
⇒ Weekly cash 4	5/24/2016	150.00	0.00
⇒ Gas card	5/26/2016	320.00	0.00
⇒ Groceries 5	5/31/2016	130.00	0.00
⇒ Weekly cash 5	5/31/2016	150.00	0.00
⇒ House payment	5/31/2016	925.00	0.00
⊟ Credit Cards / Misc			
⇒ Furniture ($2350)	5/7/2016	25.00	0.00
⇒ Charge 1 ($755)	5/15/2016	15.00	0.00
⇒ Charge 2 ($4500)	5/31/2016	50.00	0.00
⊟ Projects			
⇒ FG1 - Cash Stash	5/31/2016	250.00	0.00
⇒ FG2 - Grand Reserves	5/31/2016	200.25	0.00
⊟ Unbudgeted			

FIGURE 8-2

Notice how the Smiths labeled their goals as FG1 and FG2 to help them see where they are in terms of completing their goals. Notice also that the Smiths planned for these goals to be paid on the last day of the month. Why is that? As you make payments and deposits, you will find that the amount you budgeted and the amount you entered as actual deposits or payments are different. Perhaps your power bill turned out to be more expensive than you expected. There are also unexpected bills such as doctor visits that come in during the month. You may have to adjust and possibly eliminate the goal entries you placed under the "Projects" category based on what extra expenses come in during the month. If you pay off these "Projects" items early, then you may not have anything else you can fall back on should you need access to more money when you start going over budget. For now, make sure all your goal entries are listed to be paid on the last day of the month. These expenses are also known as fallback expenses.

After the Smiths finished entering their expenses, it was evident that they had a balanced budget. Their total expected income equaled their total expected expenses. Their budgeted balance (income minus expenses) is zero. But do you really have to get it down to zero? That depends on how you want to operate your budget. For obvious reasons, you have to at least get to the point where your budgeted income is greater than or equal to your budgeted expenses. There are advantages and disadvantages to operating either way. One advantage of starting with a zero-balanced budget is that you will quickly see how far ahead or how far behind you are in your budget as you start to record actual income and expenses. You can then make quick decisions on what to adjust (usually those fallback expenses, such as financial goals) to get back on track. The disadvantage to this approach is that you may start the month with the expectation that you will be able to apply so much money to a project or goal, only to realize halfway through the month that the amount you can actually apply is much less because of the number of unbudgeted expenses or because budgeted expenses were costlier than expected. That can be especially frustrating for a married couple as one spouse tries to explain to the other why they aren't able to put as much toward a financial goal. You also have the extra work of having to adjust those fallback expenses to get back on track.

If you decide not to list your financial goals right away or to enter a smaller amount, you will be left with a larger initial budget balance that can be used as a safety net when unbudgeted expenses occur. The disadvantage to this approach is that you may spend the excess money more freely than you would have if the money was dedicated to a goal. There is no right or wrong answer here, so you may want to experiment with both methods to see what works best for you. In the past, I always started out with a zero balance and worked from there, but recently I have been more in favor of starting off with a positive budget balance. I've been budgeting for many years, and I ALWAYS have something unexpected or unbudgeted occur, so I like to leave a little positive balance in there to take care of such items as they occur. This practice also helps reduce the adjustments I have to make to fallback expenses such as my financial goals.

At this time, make sure *Projects* is the default category and enter any goals you want to include in your initial budget.

UNBUDGETED

The final expense category is "Unbudgeted" expenses. Since you are preparing your initial budget, everything should be budgeted, so do not make any entries in this category at this time.

One final word of advice on the Expenses: try not to forget anything! The more you leave out, the more that will be added to the "Unbudgeted" category later in the month and the more trouble you will have trying to meet your budget.

A TIME TO SHARE

You've done it! You've created a balanced budget with no cash flow problems, and now you are ready to tackle the month. Well, almost ready. You need to get final acceptance of your budget from anyone else in your family who needs to understand how the money is going to be spent. Make sure your significant other understands, supports, and has input on the initial budget. He or she may know of some expense that you forgot to write down or may have different ideas on how to use the excess income. Either way, you don't want to bypass this critical step—unless, of course, you're single.

The great thing about the *Budget Ninjas* system is that it's online, which means others can access your budget from anywhere to see where things stand. There are a couple of ways you can give others the ability to view or update your budget. You could give your user name and password to your significant other so he or she can log in and work with the budget just like you. That person might also register for his or her own account, and establish a blank budget used simply to link to your budget. This is explained in more detail in *Week 10 – Connect Features*.

Having balanced your budget and verified that your cash flow is positive, you can now take a breather, sit back, and relax. The hard part is done—putting together a mutually agreed upon plan of what you are proposing to earn and spend for the month. Now comes the other hard part: sticking to the plan and working your budget.

WORKING YOUR BUDGET

Just because you have a balanced budget in hand doesn't mean you can tiptoe through the tulips until next month. You've got to work that budget. As the month progresses, you will be paying bills, withdrawing money, and making deposits into your checking account. You need to record these transactions into your budget so that you can accurately gauge how well you are sticking to the plan. Staying as close as you can to your budget takes real discipline. Don't be surprised if in the first few months you find yourself wavering with a truckload of unbudgeted expenses. However, if you are serious, then you need discipline if you want to achieve the goals you have written down, such as eliminating debt, taking a vacation, or buying that house you have always dreamed about.

Working the budget is easy. About once a week, go back through all the transactions you recorded in your checkbook since the last time you updated your budget. You need to record the actual details of deposits and expenses that hit your account. That means updating the "actual" column in your budget with what really happened. It could also mean you need to add a new income or expense entry that you weren't expecting—the dreaded unbudgeted expense. As the month progresses and more actual amounts are recorded, you will start to see the overall impact to your budget. You might want to update your budget only once a week, which is what I do most of the time. Just be aware that the system is going to say you have some entries that need to be made when you log back in. If your budget is tight, you might want to keep a closer watch on it, perhaps even daily until you get over the rough period. We'll let you know if we detect that things are going to get tight later in the month. That's good information to know ahead of time because you'll think twice before blowing money on something frivolous if you know your cash is already running low.

If this is your first update, start from the point in your checkbook at which you wrote your "In Bank" entry. For the Smiths, it is already May 15th, and as you can see in Figure 8-3, there has been a lot of activity in their budget. They have updated some income and expense entries and have even added an unbudgeted expense.

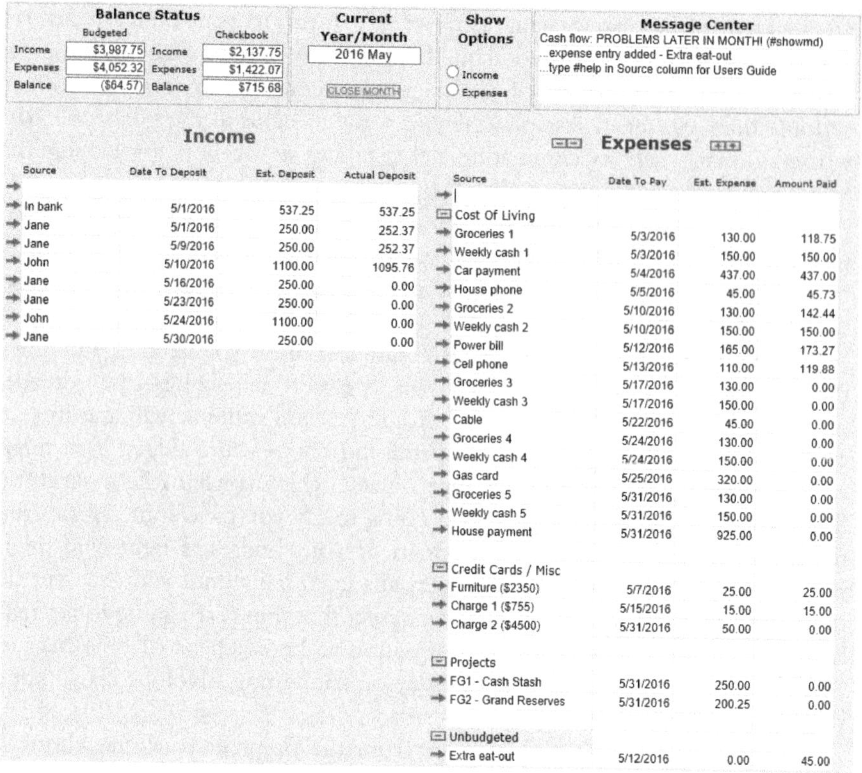

DENNIS K. BYRD

FIGURE 8-3

The system has recalculated their budgeted income and expenses based on what was deposited and left to deposit, and what was paid, and left to be paid. They see their budgeted balance is negative now and the *Message Center* has picked up on the issue. This illustrates the problem with budgeting every penny you have at the beginning of the month: when you go a little over budget, you then have to adjust those fallback expenses to get your budget back on track. At least with the *Budget Ninjas* system, you know exactly how much you need to adjust, but it's still additional work. They also see that they currently have $715.68 in the bank. This matches their checkbook so they feel confident that they didn't forget anything.

Looking at the *Income* area, we can see that both John and Jane were close on their estimates of how much their paycheck deposits were going to be. Jane made a few dollars more and John made a few dollars less. They also did well in avoiding the potential cash flow shortage on the 7th and 8th day of the month. They splurged a little and ran out of their weekly cash on Week 2, but they still went out to eat at a nice restaurant, spending $45. Now they

128

have their first unbudgeted expense. Notice that the estimated amount for the unbudgeted entry was left at $0.00 and only an actual amount was entered.

The Smiths are now considered "over budget". They have spent more than they expected to have to spend. So how do the Smiths correct this problem? They go back through the budget balancing exercise. They either need to increase income or to decrease remaining expenses. For the Smiths, this is a quick fix as they simply reduce the amount they were going to set aside for their "grand" reserves as shown in Figure 8-4.

Balance Status			Current Year/Month	Show Options	Message Center
	Budgeted	Checkbook	2016 May		Cash flow: Great!
Income	$3,987.75 Income	$2,137.75		○ Income	...expense entry updated - FG2 - Grand Reserves
Expenses	$3,987.75 Expenses	$1,422.07		○ Expenses	...expense entry updated - FG2 - Grand Reserves
Balance	$0.00 Balance	$715.68	CLOSE MONTH		...type #help in Source column for Users Guide

Income

Source	Date To Deposit	Est. Deposit	Actual Deposit
In bank	5/1/2016	537.25	537.25
Jane	5/1/2016	250.00	252.37
Jane	5/9/2016	250.00	252.37
John	5/10/2016	1100.00	1095.76
Jane	5/16/2016	250.00	0.00
Jane	5/23/2016	250.00	0.00
John	5/24/2016	1100.00	0.00
Jane	5/30/2016	250.00	0.00

Expenses

Source	Date To Pay	Est. Expense	Amount Paid
Cost Of Living			
Groceries 1	5/3/2016	130.00	118.75
Weekly cash 1	5/3/2016	150.00	150.00
Car payment	5/4/2016	437.00	437.00
House phone	5/5/2016	45.00	45.73
Groceries 2	5/10/2016	130.00	142.44
Weekly cash 2	5/10/2016	150.00	150.00
Power bill	5/12/2016	165.00	173.27
Cell phone	5/13/2016	110.00	119.88
Groceries 3	5/17/2016	130.00	0.00
Weekly cash 3	5/17/2016	150.00	0.00
Cable	5/22/2016	45.00	0.00
Groceries 4	5/24/2016	130.00	0.00
Weekly cash 4	5/24/2016	150.00	0.00
Gas card	5/25/2016	320.00	0.00
Groceries 5	5/31/2016	130.00	0.00
Weekly cash 5	5/31/2016	150.00	0.00
House payment	5/31/2016	925.00	0.00
Credit Cards / Misc			
Furniture ($2350)	5/7/2016	25.00	25.00
Charge 1 ($755)	5/15/2016	15.00	15.00
Charge 2 ($4500)	5/31/2016	50.00	0.00
Projects			
FG1 - Cash Stash	5/31/2016	250.00	0.00
FG2 - Grand Reserves	5/31/2016	135.68	0.00
Unbudgeted			
Extra eat-out	5/12/2016	0.00	45.00

FIGURE 8-4

The Smiths had to reduce the amount they were planning to put into their "grand" reserves by the $64.57 they were behind in their budget, and now they only have $135.68 they can put toward the "grand" reserves. This lets you see what kind of impact extra spending can have on achieving your goals. The Smiths may need to make more adjustments later as more bills are paid and they discover how far behind (or ahead) they are in their budget.

If you are behind in your budget by more than the total of your remaining fallback items, then you need to be concerned. You will probably want to watch your remaining expenses closely and make sure the difference is made up so that all bills can be paid, either by decreasing remaining expenses or increasing income.

If you show a positive budget balance, good for you! You may want to treat yourself to an unbudgeted surprise or treat—but don't spend more than the balance! In fact, you may want to hold off until you get closer to the end of the month, when you are sure you are going to have a positive balance remaining.

Repeat this process at least once a week, entering actual amounts for

Balance Status			
	Budgeted		Checkbook
Income	$3,987.75	Income	$2,137.75
Expenses	$3,987.75	Expenses	$1,422.07
Balance	$0.00	Balance	$715.68

expenses and income as they occur, making sure your checkbook balance matches your actual physical checkbook balance. If it doesn't, either you have forgotten to record an entry in your budget that you recorded in your checkbook, you have written down the wrong amount, or you have made an adding or subtracting mistake in your checkbook. Check your entries and make sure everything matches and the math is good. Doing this a couple of times a month has certainly helped me keep my checkbook in balance. As for the Smiths, they have deposited a total of $2137.75 and paid out a total of $1422.07 so far this month, and they have a checkbook balance of $715.68. They have also verified that this amount matches what is shown in their checkbook.

Pay close attention to the messages in the message center. If a date goes by and you haven't updated and income or expense entry with the actual amount, the message center will let you know how many need updating.

One of my favorite commands is the #OE command. This command will filter your budget so only outstanding entries are shown. This is extremely helpful when you only want to focus on income entries not yet deposited and expense entries not yet paid. Here is what their budget looks like after entering the #OE command as shown in Figure 8-5. In order to show all budget entries again, issue the command #AE to show all entries. Also, if you want to turn your focus to only the completed entries, you can issue the #CE command.

	Balance Status			Current Year/Month	Show Options	Message Center
	Budgeted		Checkbook			Cash flow: Great!
Income	$3,987.75	Income	$2,137.75	2016 May		...showing only outstanding budget entries
Expenses	$3,987.75	Expenses	$1,422.07		○ Income	...type #help in Source column for Users Guide
Balance	$0.00	Balance	$715.68	CLOSE MONTH	○ Expenses	

Income

Source	Date To Deposit	Est. Deposit	Actual Deposit
➡			
➡ Jane	5/16/2016	250.00	0.00
➡ Jane	5/23/2016	250.00	0.00
➡ John	5/24/2016	1100.00	0.00
➡ Jane	5/30/2016	250.00	0.00

Expenses

Source	Date To Pay	Est. Expense	Amount Paid
➡			
⊟ Cost Of Living			
➡ Groceries 3	5/17/2016	130.00	0.00
➡ Weekly cash 3	5/17/2016	150.00	0.00
➡ Cable	5/22/2016	45.00	0.00
➡ Groceries 4	5/24/2016	130.00	0.00
➡ Weekly cash 4	5/24/2016	150.00	0.00
➡ Gas card	5/25/2016	320.00	0.00
➡ Groceries 5	5/31/2016	130.00	0.00
➡ Weekly cash 5	5/31/2016	150.00	0.00
➡ House payment	5/31/2016	925.00	0.00
⊟ Credit Cards / Misc			
➡ Charge 2 ($4500)	5/31/2016	50.00	0.00
⊟ Projects			
➡ FG1 - Cash Stash	5/31/2016	250.00	0.00
➡ FG2 - Grand Reserves	5/31/2016	135.68	0.00
⊟ Unbudgeted			

FIGURE 8-5

A TIME TO SHARE - AGAIN

Since you have done this work, now is the perfect time to give your other family members an update on the budget. If you were way off and had to make some drastic changes, make sure you communicate what happened. Your budget should have all the information and details that describe how you got off track. Discuss ways to improve the process and get back on track, and ask for their ideas. Constant communication is the key. If you wait until the end of the month to dump all the bad news on them, the emotional impact is likely to be higher. Use the budget to your advantage as you work it. One of its purposes is to keep you out of trouble! Hopefully, you'll have good news to share instead as your budget helps you stay on track and you are able to make progress toward your goals.

CLOSING YOUR BUDGET

It is now the end of the month, and you are sitting down paying your remaining bills. Closing your budget simply means you pay your final expenses for the month and setup your budget for the next month. There are a couple of additional items you need to consider before you pay those final bills, though. First of all, you should pay those fallback expenses last, if at all possible. The Smiths had two fallback expenses—the money to take out for their cash stash, and the money to put toward their "grand" reserves. Go ahead and pay your remaining bills for the month, but leave your fallback expenses unpaid if you have any. The Smiths paid their final bills and here was where they stood as shown in Figure 8-6.

Balance Status				Current	Show	Message Center
Budgeted		Checkbook		Year/Month	Options	Cash flow: Great!
Income	$4,106.04	Income	$4,106.04	2016 May		...expense entry added - School field trip
Expenses	$4,037.47	Expenses	$3,651.79		○ Income	...expense entry updated - Charge 2 ($4500)
Balance	$68.57	Balance	$454.25		○ Expenses	...expense entry updated - House payment
				CLOSE MONTH		...expense entry updated - Weekly cash 5

Income

Source	Date To Deposit	Est. Deposit	Actual Deposit
In bank	5/1/2016	537.25	537.25
Jane	5/1/2016	250.00	252.37
Jane	5/9/2016	250.00	252.37
John	5/10/2016	1100.00	1095.76
Jane	5/16/2016	250.00	252.37
Jane	5/23/2016	250.00	307.33
John	5/24/2016	1100.00	1095.75
Jane	5/30/2016	250.00	312.84

Expenses

Source	Date To Pay	Est. Expense	Amount Paid
Cost Of Living			
Groceries 1	5/3/2016	130.00	118.75
Weekly cash 1	5/3/2016	150.00	150.00
Car payment	5/4/2016	437.00	437.00
House phone	5/5/2016	45.00	45.73
Groceries 2	5/10/2016	130.00	142.44
Weekly cash 2	5/10/2016	150.00	150.00
Power bill	5/12/2016	165.00	173.27
Cell phone	5/13/2016	110.00	119.88
Groceries 3	5/17/2016	130.00	117.11
Weekly cash 3	5/17/2016	150.00	150.00
Cable	5/22/2016	45.00	44.79
Groceries 4	5/24/2016	130.00	143.22
Weekly cash 4	5/24/2016	150.00	150.00
Gas card	5/25/2016	320.00	365.92
Groceries 5	5/31/2016	130.00	118.68
Weekly cash 5	5/31/2016	150.00	150.00
House payment	5/31/2016	925.00	925.00
Credit Cards / Misc			
Furniture ($2350)	5/7/2016	25.00	25.00
Charge 1 ($755)	5/15/2016	15.00	15.00
Charge 2 ($4500)	5/31/2016	50.00	50.00
Projects			
FG1 - Cash Stash	5/31/2016	250.00	0.00
FG2 - Grand Reserves	5/31/2016	135.68	0.00
Unbudgeted			
Extra eat-out	5/12/2016	0.00	45.00
School field trip	5/18/2016	0.00	15.00

FIGURE 8-6

You can see they had another unbudgeted expense (school field trip), but Jane brought in a little extra money by working some overtime. They are pleased to find that they are now ahead in their budget by $68.57. They have $454.25 left in their checkbook, which is more than the two remaining fallback expenses to be paid. Now they need to make some decisions. The Smiths want to withdraw $250.00 so they have their cash stash, which would leave them with $204.25 in their checking account. However, they remember they almost ran out of money for a couple of days last month, so they decide to leave the whole $454.25 in checking until they are able to build up their "grand" reserves enough that they don't have cash flow problems anymore.

The Smiths are now ready to start work on next month's budget. To me, this is the most valuable feature of the *Budget Ninjas* system. Closing your budget is not some complex accounting process that you need a CPA to perform. All you have to do to close your budget is copy your entries from the current month to the next month so you do not have to re-enter all of them. This is a huge time saver. Double check that your checkbook ending balance for the month matches what you currently have in your checkbook. Then click the *Close Month* button in the *Current Year/Month* section. You will see something similar to the following as shown in Figure 8-7.

Balance Status			Current Year/Month	Show Options	Message Center
	Budgeted	Checkbook	2016 May		Cash flow: Great!
Income	$4,106.04	Income $4,106.04		○ Income	...type #help in Source column for Users Guide
Expenses	$4,037.47	Expenses $3,651.79		○ Expenses	
Balance	$68.57	Balance $454.25	CLOSE MONTH		

Close The Month

Items Checked Are Copied

Close a month to copy entries in the current month to the next month. Use the grid on the right to choose which expense items should be copied. All income entries will be copied. Dates will automatically be adjusted for you for the next month. Any entries already present in the next month will remain untouched. If you are using the linked budgets feature, you, or the person you are linked to, will need to perform a separate close for each budget. Unbudgeted entries selected will be moved to the Credit Cards / Miscellaneous category on the next month (you can change category later). After the process completes, the next month will be displayed and you can adjust entries accordingly for items copied.

Press "Proceed" when you are ready, or "Back" if you are not yet ready.

Proceed

Back

Source	Date To Pay	Est. Expense	Amount Paid
Cost Of Living			
☑ Groceries 1	5/3/2016	130.00	118.75
☑ Weekly cash 1	5/3/2016	150.00	150.00
☑ Car payment	5/4/2016	437.00	437.00
☑ House phone	5/5/2016	45.00	45.73
☑ Groceries 2	5/10/2016	130.00	142.44
☑ Weekly cash 2	5/10/2016	150.00	150.00
☑ Power bill	5/12/2016	165.00	173.27
☑ Cell phone	5/13/2016	110.00	119.88
☑ Groceries 3	5/17/2016	130.00	117.11
☑ Weekly cash 3	5/17/2016	150.00	150.00
☑ Cable	5/22/2016	45.00	44.79
☑ Groceries 4	5/24/2016	130.00	143.22
☑ Weekly cash 4	5/24/2016	150.00	150.00
☑ Gas card	5/25/2016	320.00	365.92
☑ Groceries 5	5/31/2016	130.00	118.68
☑ Weekly cash 5	5/31/2016	150.00	150.00
☑ House payment	5/31/2016	925.00	925.00
Credit Cards / Misc			
☑ Furniture ($2350)	5/7/2016	25.00	25.00
☑ Charge 1 ($755)	5/15/2016	15.00	15.00
☑ Charge 2 ($4500)	5/31/2016	50.00	50.00
Projects			
☑ FG1 - Cash Stash	5/31/2016	250.00	0.00
☑ FG2 - Grand Reserves	5/31/2016	135.68	0.00
Unbudgeted			
☐ Extra eat-out	5/12/2016	0.00	45.00
☐ School field trip	5/18/2016	0.00	15.00

FIGURE 8-7

All your income entries are copied. TIP! If you spell your "In Bank" entry just like this, we will automatically update the values for it to show the amount of money you currently have in the bank.

You are presented with a list of all your expenses for the month with a checkbox beside each one. All of them are checked by default, with the exception of the unbudgeted expenses. We are guessing that these types of expenses are not likely to be repeated, so we leave them unchecked. If you do check an unbudgeted expense, it will be copied to the next month, but we'll move it to the "Credit Cards/Misc." category. You can always move it to a different category later if you want. If the expense is going to be repeated, make sure you have it checked so it is copied over. We'll change the date for you to the same day on the next month. You might have to go in and make a few adjustments after the fact, but this process sure does beat having to re-enter all this information.

Press "Proceed" to complete the copy, and the system will work its magic and move you to the next month as shown in Figure 8-8.

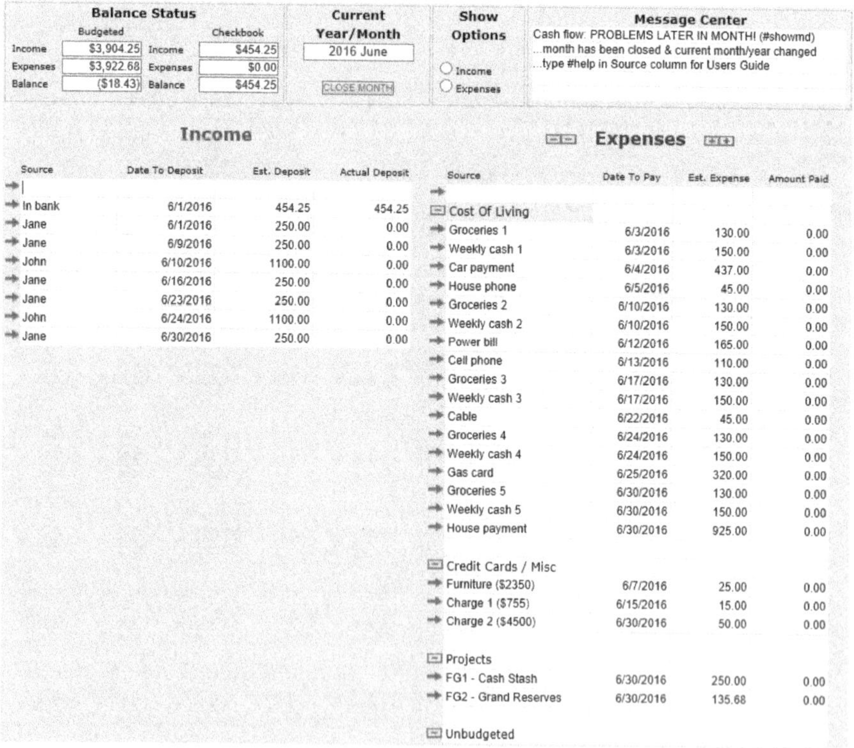

FIGURE 8-8

134

Notice that all the actual amounts have been reset to zero for you with the exception of the "In Bank" entry. Also, all the dates have changed to the same day on the next month. An exception to this is that if you had an entry for the 31st day of the month, the entry will be added to the last day of the next month, which could be the 30th, or the 28th or 29th if in February. Verify that your "In Bank" entry reflects the current amount you have in the bank. Now all you have to do is make some adjustments here and there and you'll be finished preparing next month's budget in no time.

If you decide you really want some of those items you didn't check in the previous month, it's not too late. Navigate back to the previous month and click the *Close Month* button again. Make sure you uncheck the entries you don't want and check the entries you forgot the first time you closed. Only the new entries are copied. As long as you haven't changed the dates on any of your existing entries in the new month, the system will not duplicate those because it realizes they are already in the next month. Still, you might want to double check just to be sure. Also, the system will remember the tags you placed, so you don't have to worry about retagging anything either.

As the months progress, your budget will become more and more precise and you will gain better control of your finances. This is your ultimate goal—you controlling your finances, not your finances controlling you. After you close the budget for the month, make sure you communicate with your family the final status for the month, informing them of progress made on goals, explaining where unbudgeted expenses came from, and asking for advice and ideas for the next month. Repeat the process, and soon you will be a budget hero!

WEEK 8 – QUESTIONS & DISCUSSION
(You may copy this page as needed)

1. If you have more income than expenses, is it possible to have bad cash flow? Why or why not?

   _____

   _____

   _____

2. Explain what a fallback expense is, and why they are so important.

   _____

   _____

   _____

3. What's the advantage of starting off with a zero balanced budget (projected income equals projected expenses)?

   _____

   _____

   _____

4. TRUE or FALSE.
   Use the Unbudgeted category to enter expenses that you don't really want to include in your budget, but might have to pay anyway.

5. What command can you issue to only show outstanding budget entries? How would you then show all entries?

   _____

6. What's the dis-advantage of starting off with a zero balanced budget (projected income equals projected expenses)?

   _____

   _____

   _____

WEEK 9 – WORKING YOUR GOALS

In week 4, we talked about your goals and recommended you work on the following financial goals until they are achieved. By "work on", we mean including expense items in your budget under the Projects category. Most likely, you will have to work on one at a time, and it may take several months just to complete one goal. To review, here is the list of financial goals, and the order in which they should be completed:

FINANCIAL GOAL #1 – YOUR CASH STASH
FINANCIAL GOAL #2 – YOUR "GRAND" RESERVES
FINANCIAL GOAL #3 – LARGE RECURRING HEADACHES
FINANCIAL GOAL #4 – GETTING CAUGHT UP
FINANCIAL GOAL #5 – MUCH-NEEDED REPAIRS
FINANCIAL GOAL #6 – FREE MONEY
FINANCIAL GOAL #7 – SHORT-TERM SUCCESS
FINANCIAL GOAL #8 – WORKING RESERVES
FINANCIAL GOAL #9 – THE LONG HAUL

Review week 4 again if you need more details about each individual goal. We also keep this material available directly from your budget through our online #help. Access #help by issuing the command, and then click on the *Ninja Goals Index* button. Each goal is displayed (see Figure 9-1). Click the arrow beside the goal you want to review.

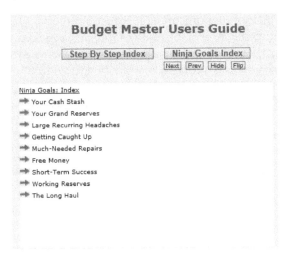

FIGURE 9-1

Financial goals #1, #4, #5 are easy enough to integrate into your budget as you would simply enter the expense amounts for these directly into your budget.

For financial goals #2, #3, and #8, you may want to use the project tracking tool available from the *Connect* page, called *My Projects*.

MY PROJECTS

Navigate to the *Connect* page. You will see three tabs: My Connections, My Budgets, and My Projects. Click on My Projects. The following is displayed (Figure 9-2).

FIGURE 9-2

My Projects is an integrated financial planning tool that provides maximum flexibility for you to decide how you are going to achieve your financial goals. The tool supports multiple expense projects (such as trips of a lifetime), with automatic leveling of reserves (savings) required with ability to increase/decrease those savings on individual months as needed. Once your project is set, everything is included in your budget month after month to ensure your project is a success.

The Smiths have been dreaming about taking an anniversary trip to Venice, Italy but have never been able to save enough money to achieve such a dream. For fun, they will create a new project to see what kind of impact a trip like that would have on their budget. Follow along as well creating your own dream vacation. First order of business is trying to determine all the costs associated with such a trip. The Smiths have identified the following expenses (although in reality, I'm sure there are more):

Passport - $250
Airline tickets - $2,200
Hotel - $1,000
Spending money - $750

Some of these expenses will need to be paid before the others, like getting the passports and ordering the airline tickets. Click on the NEW Project button to start building your dream vacation. The following is displayed.

Create New Project

Description: Venice

Budget: Johns ▾

Enter 2 of the following to create your initial plan:

Total goal: 750.00 ×

Monthly goal:

Target date: 5/15/2017

NOTE: We'll calculate the remaining value for you based on the other two values you enter. We'll also ignore target date if you enter all three values. If you enter a target date, it should be the date you expect to have to pay the last bill for this project. You'll be able to fine-tune your project plan after you build it.

Build It   Back

FIGURE 9-3

There are a number of ways to setup your project. Most projects, like establishing your Grand Reserves, will contain a single expense, and the name you give your project would match the description of that expense. However, for projects that contain multiple expenses, you want to start with the last expense that would be paid and use a general description that represents the entire project. For the Smiths, their last expense is spending money in the amount of $750. They enter "Venice" as their project description, and $750 as the goal for their last expense. They are hoping to go in May of 2017, so they select the date they want the trip to begin. When they press the *"Build It"* button, the initial project is built and displayed as follows (example assumes date project built was December, 2015 – see Figure 9-4).

| My Budgets | My Projects | My Account |

NEW Project

Projects	Description	Goal	Progress	Months Left
Options	Venice	750.00	0.00	18

FIGURE 9-4

The project summary display informs you of the current state of each project. For the Smiths, we currently see the goal of $750 (which we'll change as we add more expenses to the project), and that they have 18 months left to achieve that goal, with no progress made yet.

You can have multiple projects running at the same time. Each one is listed here so you can easily see the status and choose the one you want to work with.

Click on Options to display more details about the project. The following is displayed (Figure 9-5).

My Budgets	My Projects	My Account					

What do you want to do with: Venice

Option 1 Add Expense
Option 2 Delete Project
Option 3 Override Reserves
Option 4 Update Expense
Option 5 Delete Expense

Back

Projects	Description		Goal	Progress	Months Left
Options	Venice		750.00	0.00	18

Projects Detail	Expense Description	Date	Budgeted Expenses	Monthly Reserves	Reserve Balance
Options		2015-12-31		44.12	44.12
Options		2016-01-31		44.12	88.24
Options		2016-02-29		44.12	132.36
Options		2016-03-31		44.12	176.48
Options		2016-04-30		44.12	220.60
Options		2016-05-31		44.12	264.72
Options		2016-06-30		44.12	308.84
Options		2016-07-31		44.12	352.96
Options		2016-08-31		44.12	397.08
Options		2016-09-30		44.12	441.20
Options		2016-10-31		44.12	485.32
Options		2016-11-30		44.12	529.44
Options		2016-12-31		44.12	573.56
Options		2017-01-31		44.12	617.68
Options		2017-02-28		44.12	661.80
Options		2017-03-31		44.12	705.92
Options		2017-04-30		44.08	750.00
Options	Venice	2017-05-15	750.00		0.00

FIGURE 9-5

The system has calculated how much reserves (savings) is needed each month in order to meet the initial goal of having $750 spending money when the trip starts. Currently, we'll need $44.12 per month for 18 months to come up with $750. Notice how the reserve balance continues to accumulate until the expense is paid. Also notice that our expense description is the same as our project description. For single expense projects, that's fine, but in our example, we will end up with multiple expenses so we need to change the description of that expense. Click *Options* beside the Venice expense, click Option 4 to update the expense, and then give your expense a better description.

Next, we want to add in the expense for the passports. *Click on Option 1 – Add Expense button.* The following is displayed (Figure 9-6).

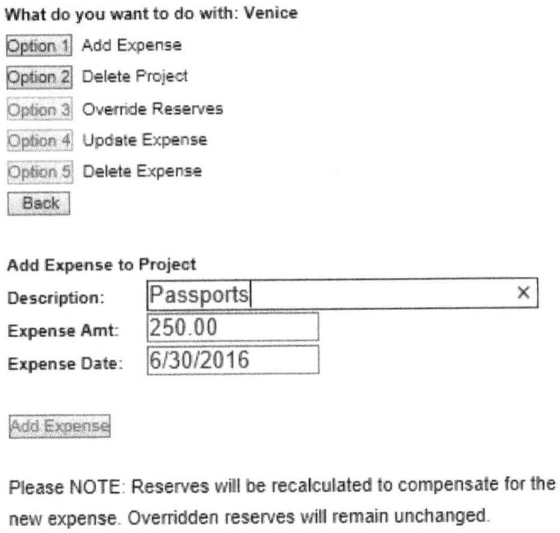

What do you want to do with: Venice

Option 1	Add Expense
Option 2	Delete Project
Option 3	Override Reserves
Option 4	Update Expense
Option 5	Delete Expense
Back	

Add Expense to Project

Description:	Passports ×
Expense Amt:	250.00
Expense Date:	6/30/2016

Add Expense

Please NOTE: Reserves will be recalculated to compensate for the new expense. Overridden reserves will remain unchanged.

FIGURE 9-6

Enter the description of the new expense, the expense amount, and the date the expense is to be paid. Then press the *Add Expense* button. As noted, the reserves will be recalculated to compensate for the new expense. The Smiths went ahead and added the other expenses too and used the update expense option to change the description of their last expense to "Spending Money". Here is how their project looks now (Figure 9-7).

| My Budgets | My Projects | My Account |

NEW Project

Projects	Description		Goal	Progress	Months Left
Options	Venice		4,200.00	0.00	18

Projects Detail	Expense Description	Date	Budgeted Expenses	Monthly Reserves	Reserve Balance
Options		2015-12-31		272.22	272.22
Options		2016-01-31		272.22	544.44
Options		2016-02-29		272.22	816.66
Options		2016-03-31		272.22	1,088.88
Options		2016-04-30		272.22	1,361.10
Options		2016-05-31		272.22	1,633.32
Options	Passports	2016-06-30	250.00		1,383.32
Options		2016-06-30		272.22	1,655.54
Options		2016-07-31		272.22	1,927.76
Options		2016-08-31		272.24	2,200.00
Options	Airline Tickets	2016-09-19	2,200.00		0.00
Options		2016-09-30		218.75	218.75
Options		2016-10-31		218.75	437.50
Options		2016-11-30		218.75	656.25
Options		2016-12-31		218.75	875.00
Options		2017-01-31		218.75	1,093.75
Options		2017-02-28		218.75	1,312.50
Options		2017-03-31		218.75	1,531.25
Options		2017-04-30		218.75	1,750.00
Options	Spending money	2017-05-15	750.00		1,000.00
Options	Hotel	2017-05-15	1,000.00		0.00

FIGURE 9-7

Our new total project goal is now $4,200. Notice how the monthly reserve amounts adjust automatically to insure the expenses can be paid as they come due. Notice also how the reserve balance is used to pay for the expenses. The real impact to your budget is the amount of monthly reserves the system calculates you will need in order to pay for these expenses.

The final adjustment the Smiths will make is overriding the reserves in March. He is expecting a bonus as well as a sizable income tax refund and wants to use some of that money for the trip. He overrides the reserves to $800. To overrride reserves, click the Options button beside the month you want to override (not an actual expense though), and click option 3 to override the reserves. Enter the new amount you want to reserve for that month (could be more, or could be less, depending on what you need to do). If you later change your mind and want to remove that override, click Option

3 again and click the option to remove the override. Look at the impact that change had to the reserves needed each month for the Smiths (see Figure 9-8).

| My Budgets | My Projects | My Account |

NEW Project

Projects	Description		Goal	Progress	Months Left
Options	Venice		4,200.00	0.00	18

Projects Detail	Expense Description	Date	Budgeted Expenses	Monthly Reserves	Reserve Balance
Options		2015-12-31		212.50	212.50
Options		2016-01-31		212.50	425.00
Options		2016-02-29		212.50	637.50
Options		2016-03-31		800.00	1,437.50
Options		2016-04-30		212.50	1,650.00
Options		2016-05-31		212.50	1,862.50
Options	Passports	2016-06-30	250.00		1,612.50
Options		2016-06-30		212.50	1,825.00
Options		2016-07-31		212.50	2,037.50
Options		2016-08-31		212.50	2,250.00
Options	Airline Tickets	2016-09-19	2,200.00		50.00
Options		2016-09-30		212.50	262.50
Options		2016-10-31		212.50	475.00
Options		2016-11-30		212.50	687.50
Options		2016-12-31		212.50	900.00
Options		2017-01-31		212.50	1,112.50
Options		2017-02-28		212.50	1,325.00
Options		2017-03-31		212.50	1,537.50
Options		2017-04-30		212.50	1,750.00
Options	Spending money	2017-05-15	750.00		1,000.00
Options	Hotel	2017-05-15	1,000.00		0.00

FIGURE 9-8

The amount of monthly reserves needed for the other months have been considerably reduced based on the additional money applied in March through the overriden reserves.

What kind of impact does a project like this now have on the budget? Looking at the above, they essentially need to set aside $212.50 a month (extra in March as planned). If we were to look at their budget in June, we should see an expense of $250 to pay the passport, and another expense of

143

$1825.00 which is the total of all their reserves remaining that have been accumulating thus far (see Figure 9-9).

Projects			
Passports	6/30/2016	250.00	0.00
Reserves-Venice	6/30/2016	1825.00	0.00

FIGURE 9-9

The expenses from My Projects will appear in green color in your budget. That means the values cannot be adjusted here. The only piece that can be entered is the actual amount paid for the Passports. Based on the amount that is actually paid, the system will automatically adjust remaining reserve entries for you. How cool is that! A system like this makes it extremely difficult to fail in completing your projects.

Since the reserve expenses cannot be paid, the intent is to leave that money in your checking account and let it accumulate month after month. Your beginning "In bank" income entry for each month will grow and grow as your reserves continue to grow. As expenses are paid, the reserves will be reduced by that amount until all the reserves are consumed when the last check is written for the project. Having projects like this in your budget helps eliminate other cash flow issues as well.

If you are just experimenting, you can delete the project when you are finished playing with the numbers.

For your Grand Reserves and Working Reserves, you may want to approach your project a little differently. Instead of entering a date that you want the project completed by, enter the amount of money you can spare each month, along with the total goal, and let the system determine when you will be able to meet that goal. That way, you wont have the stress of trying to come up with unrealistic amounts of money each month.

The great thing about My Projects is the flexibility. If you have a bad month of expenses, go into your project on that month and override the reserves, reducing the amount you can handle that month. The system will recalculate what it needs in the remaining months. If you have to move expenses out a few months, that's ok too! At least now you have the tools to manage progress and can quickly get back on track.

SHORT TERM SUCCESS

Let's turn our focus now to Financial Goal #7 – Short-Term Success. Now that you have a good, working budget, how do you go about getting rid of all that debt? Half the battle is getting on a budget and staying on a budget. If you haven't made good progress on the previous financial goals, like setting aside money for your cash stash and building your "grand" reserves, I would wait until you do before jumping in headfirst to eliminate debt, although it is very tempting now that you have a budget in your hand. If you remember, one of the steps you performed when balancing your budget was to initially apply only the minimum balances to your charge cards. With prior goals under control, if you still find you have more budgeted income than expenses, you can now decide which debt you would like to get rid of first. Your ability to decide what credit cards or loans to apply the extra money to is the key to quickly coming out of debt. Without a budget, you would probably spend any excess income on other items which may or may not be necessary, and you would make only the minimum payment required by the charge company, making little progress toward getting out of debt.

Working your way out of debt is not an easy pill to swallow. It really does take discipline to stick to your budget to ensure that you can apply as much money as possible to this goal. It takes time to accumulate debt, and it will take time to eliminate it. Communication becomes especially important as you embark on such a quest. If one of you has your mind set on getting out of debt while the other is still freely spending, you need to sit down together and have a good heart-to-heart conversation on what you would like to accomplish. It may be helpful to explain your desired achievement's end result, which is having more cash available for doing the things you really want to do.

Oddly enough, the process of working your way out of debt is quite simple. Again, half the work is preparing a budget so you can make the quality decisions required to get you out of debt. It is also relatively easy to determine how long it will take you to get out of debt, assuming you incur no further debt and your budget remains roughly the same in future months. Let's look at the sample budget the Smiths have been working on. Notice when they first filled out the *Expense* area for the "Credit Cards/Misc." category, they first entered the minimum payments required by the two charge cards and furniture loan. These debts have a combined minimum monthly payment of $90.00. Let's assume that the Smiths will have an additional $65.00 that can be applied to these, bringing the total money they can use to pay off debt per month to $155. Your first goal is to eliminate the charge card or loan that has the smallest outstanding

Credit Cards / Misc				
Furniture ($2,350)	05/07/2013	$25.00	$25.00
Charge 1 ($755)	05/15/2013	$15.00	$15.00
Charge 2 ($4,500)	05/31/2013	$50.00	$50.00

balance, which for the Smiths is Charge Card 1. They apply all excess money in their budget to this item. The minimum payment on Charge Card 1 is $15, so after adding the other $65 to that, they can make $80 payments on this loan until it is paid off. After the smallest debt is eliminated, start working on the new lowest balance. For the Smiths, that would be the furniture loan. Now they can take the $80 that they were putting toward Charge Card 1 and add that to their minimum payment for the furniture loan of $25. They can now make $105 payments on the furniture loan until it is paid off. After this debt is eliminated, continue working your way up in terms of balance.

Notice that after you eliminate each debt, you have more and more money available to get rid of the remaining debts, making the elimination that much faster! It is like a domino effect. Once you begin eliminating debt items, it becomes easier and easier to eliminate the rest. After your debt is eliminated, it's on to the next goal on your list!

Review Week 4, Financial Goal #7 to understand how to use the Accelerated Debt Payoff calculator that does all the above calculations for you.

WEEK 9 – QUESTIONS & DISCUSSION
(You may copy this page as needed)

1. Why do people have such a hard time completing goals?
   _____
   _____

2. How would life be different if all your financial goals were completed?
   _____
   _____

3. PRACTICE!
   Create a project to save $1000 in 12 months. How much monthly reserves were calculated?
   _____

4. What calculator can you use to figure out how quickly you can pay off all your loans?
   _____

5. In the past, how did you save for major expenses like vacations, new cars, etc.?
   _____
   _____
   _____

6. Instead of going through the trouble of learning how to save for major projects, why not just take out a loan and pay it back as time allows?
   _____
   _____
   _____

WEEK 10 – CONNECT FEATURES

Congratulations! You've made it to the final week. What more could we possibly teach you about budgeting that hasn't already been covered? There are a number of scenarios we haven't talked about yet, and some that we mentioned briefly in previous weeks. For example, how can a couple that has two checking accounts manage their budget? What about a couple that is engaged to be married? What happens when two budgets become one? What about those that want to provide financial counseling to others. Is there a way to provide oversight into their budget? All of these situations can be handled through the Connect panel. In week 9, you got a taste of that when you accessed My Projects from the Connect panel. Now let's dig deeper into the possibilities.

BUDGET CONNECTIONS

 Click on *Connect* link in the navigation bar to display the Connect page. The Connect Options page is shown in Figure 10-1.

Assigned To Me	Budget Name	Linked User	Linked Name	Linked User Permissions
Options	jsmith			

Not Assigned	Budget	Number
Options	Budget 0002	
Options	Budget 0003	

FIGURE 10-1

Three tabs are displayed to allow you to manage bank connections, budget connections, and project connections.

My Budgets page shows you the list of budgets to which you have access. Initially, you have one budget available for use.

WORKING WITH YOUR BUDGETS

Let's discuss some of the options available to you for each budget. Click the *Options* button beside one of your unassigned budgets if you want to give it a name and assign it to yourself.

For each budget you have assigned to yourself, you have the following options available to you (see Figure 10-2).

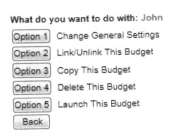

FIGURE 10-2

Option 1 – Change General Setting will allow you to do the following:

- Change your budget's name. Pick a name that is different from that of any other budget you have.
- Change the permissions you have given to your budget. If you have linked your budget with another person, you'll see an option that allows you to grant either full control or read-only permissions to your budget.
- Change your current active budget. If you have multiple budgets, you can make any one your current active budget. Anytime a new budget is launched, it automatically becomes your current active budget.

Option 2 – Link/Unlink This Budget.
We dedicate a whole section below to cover this important feature.

Option 3 – Copy This Budget will allow you to do the following:

- Make a copy of one of your budgets. You can use that copy for backup purposes, or to play what-if games. When you copy a budget, you will consume one of your available budgets. If none are available, the copy function is not allowed. You must give your copied budget a unique budget name. I use this option occasionally toward the end of the month when I want a sneak peak at what my budget is going to look like next month. I'll make a copy of my good budget and call it "Sneak Peak." Then I'll launch that copy and pretend to deposit any remaining income entries and pay out any remaining expense entries for the month I was just in. Finally, I'll close that month to see what my next month is going to look like. This comes in handy if you are trying to figure out whether you can afford to make plans for a quick trip next month or whether you are going to be able to afford that new purchase. After I've had my sneak peak, I'll return to the Connect – My Budgets page and delete the copied budget I created. Just make sure you don't delete your real budget! In fact, you might want to use the copy option to make a backup of your budget just in case you accidentally delete your real budget. A backup is also nice to have on hand if you have your budget linked to another person and he or she has full control permissions to your budget. You can use your backup, which is not linked, if you ever want to know what the budget looked like before he or she made some questionable changes.

Option 4 – Delete This Budget will allow you to do the following:
- Delete the selected budget. Use with extreme caution! At the top of the options, you'll see the comment "What do you want to do with:" Make sure the budget name listed here is really the budget you want to delete. When you select *Option 4*, we'll make you confirm that this is really what you want to do. There's no going back after the confirmation button has been pressed. If this budget was linked with anyone else, they will no longer see that they are linked to your budget. All history associated with this budget will be deleted as well.

Option 5 – Launch This Budget will allow you to do the following:
- Navigate to the Budget page with this budget. This will also change your default active budget to be the one you just launched.

LINKING BUDGETS TOGETHER

Why would you want to link budgets together? Each budget typically represents a separate bank account, and some families have multiple bank accounts that are managed separately. It is also possible that a young couple is engaged to be married and they want to learn how the other person is managing their money. Establishing a budget for each of these accounts and then linking them together allows you to see the combined view of budgeted activities over all of these accounts. This function is extremely helpful if you want to see total expenses regardless of which account is being used to pay the bill. It's also helpful when you are addressing problems that may be encountered in one account, such as cash flow issues, because it allows you to easily see whether an expense can be moved to the other account. When working with your linked budgets, you have the option to highlight one of the budgets so you can see what portion of the overall budget belongs to that particular budget.

To start the process of linking budgets together, click on *Option 2* beside a budget assigned to you. The following is displayed (see Figure 10-3).

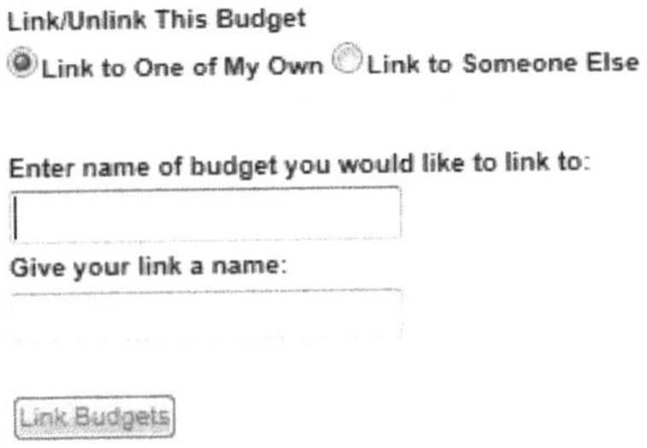

Link/Unlink This Budget
◉ Link to One of My Own ◯ Link to Someone Else

Enter name of budget you would like to link to:

Give your link a name:

[Link Budgets]

FIGURE 10-3

The default setting is to link to one of your own budgets, but you can change this setting if you want to link to a budget that belongs to someone else. If you choose that option, a few additional options are shown (see Figure 10-4).

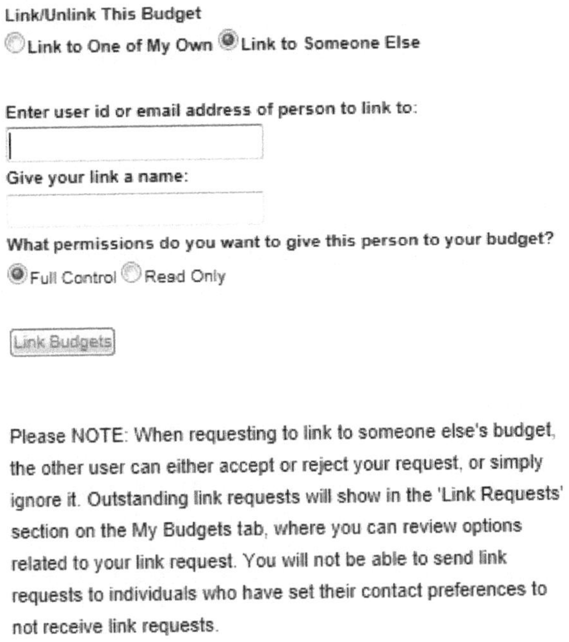

Link/Unlink This Budget
◯ Link to One of My Own ◉ Link to Someone Else

Enter user id or email address of person to link to:

Give your link a name:

What permissions do you want to give this person to your budget?
◉ Full Control ◯ Read Only

[Link Budgets]

Please NOTE: When requesting to link to someone else's budget, the other user can either accept or reject your request, or simply ignore it. Outstanding link requests will show in the 'Link Requests' section on the My Budgets tab, where you can review options related to your link request. You will not be able to send link requests to individuals who have set their contact preferences to not receive link requests.

FIGURE 10-4

Enter the name of the budget to which you want to link or the user name or email address of the person to whom you want to link. Budgets are connected by a common link name, so take the time to give your link a name. If you are linking your budget to someone else's, decide what permissions you want to give him or her. If you select Full Control, that person has full control over your budget just like you and can add, change, and delete your budget entries. If you only want the linked person to be able to see your budget entries, select Read Only.

Press the *Link Budgets* button when all selections have been made. If you are linking to another person, your link request will remain pending until he or she accepts or rejects your invitation to link, as shown here.

Assigned To Me	Budget Name	Linked User	Linked Name	Linked User Permissions
Options	John	bigcompany	Shared Business	Pending Acceptance

If you receive a pending link request, you will see it on the *My Budgets* tab, as shown here:

Link Requests	Budget Name	Request From User	Link Name	Link Permissions
Options	John	jsmith	Shared Business	Can Update

You can see who the link request came from, as well as what kind of permissions that person is willing to give if you accept the link request. Click *Options* beside a link request to either accept or decline the request. If you accept the request, you may then choose which budget you want to link to and what permissions to your budget you are going to give the other person.

You will only be able to link to one other individual for any given budget. If the budgets belong to you, however, then you can link as many of these together as you want under the same linked name.

LINKED BUDGET OPTIONS

If you noticed between the *Current Year/Month* and the *Message Center* inside

Budgets, there is a *Show Options* section that allows you to choose to display either income or expense options. When you click on the Income selection, the Income options panel is shown instead of the expense data grid. When you click on the

Expenses selection, the Expenses option panel is shown instead of the income data grid, as shown below in Figure 10-5.

Income				Options
Source	Date To Deposit	Est. Deposit	Actual Deposit	**Default budget to use when adding new entries:**
⇥ I				(NOTE: Only linked budgets shown - see admin page for more details)
⇥ In Bank	5/1/2014	537.25	537.25	John ▾
⇥ Jane	5/2/2014	250.00	0.00	
⇥ Jane	5/9/2014	250.00	0.00	**Linked Budget Filters:**
⇥ John	5/10/2014	1100.00	0.00	◉ Show entries for all linked budgets (#alb)
⇥ Jane	5/16/2014	250.00	0.00	○ Show entries for all linked budgets, highlighting selected default budget (#albh)
⇥ Jane	5/23/2014	250.00	0.00	○ Show entries only for selected default budget (#dlb)
⇥ John	5/24/2014	1100.00	0.00	
⇥ Jane	5/30/2014	250.00	0.00	**Outstanding & Completed Filters:**
				◉ Show both outstanding and completed income entries (#ae)
				○ Show only outstanding income entries (#oe)
				○ Show only completed income entries (#ce)
				[Back]

FIGURE 10-5

Whether or not this budget is linked to other budgets will determine which options are available on these panels. By default, the budget you launched will be the budget used when adding new entries, but you can change that default here if you are linked to other budgets. If you do not have full update rights to the other budget, then the only purpose for this selection is to be able to highlight that person's budget entries using the Linked Budget Filters. By default, the Linked Budget Filters section is set to show all entries from all linked budgets. If John and Jane had separate accounts and separate budgets but linked them together, it would be easy to tell which budget entries belonged to the other. They would select the budget they want to highlight and then choose the second linked budget filter, "Show entries for all linked budgets, highlighting selected default budget," as shown in Figure 10-6.

Income				Options
Source	Date To Deposit	Est. Deposit	Actual Deposit	**Default budget to use when adding new entries:**
⇥ I				(NOTE: Only linked budgets shown - see admin page for more details)
⇥ In Bank	5/1/2014	537.25	537.25	Jane ▾
⇥ Jane	5/2/2014	250.00	0.00	
⇥ Jane	5/9/2014	250.00	0.00	**Linked Budget Filters:**
⇥ John	5/10/2014	1100.00	0.00	○ Show entries for all linked budgets (#alb)
⇥ Jane	5/16/2014	250.00	0.00	◉ Show entries for all linked budgets, highlighting selected default budget (#albh)
⇥ Jane	5/23/2014	250.00	0.00	○ Show entries only for selected default budget (#dlb)
⇥ John	5/24/2014	1100.00	0.00	
⇥ Jane	5/30/2014	250.00	0.00	**Outstanding & Completed Filters:**
				◉ Show both outstanding and completed income entries (#ae)
				○ Show only outstanding income entries (#oe)
				○ Show only completed income entries (#ce)
				[Back]

FIGURE 10-6

The third linked budget filter, "Show entries only for selected default budget," is handy if you just want to focus on one budget. When you choose that option, the *Balance Status* and *Message Center* will only reflect information as it pertains to the budget selected. The main purpose of linking budgets together is so you can get a complete picture of your finances across all your accounts, but with these filters, you still have the flexibility to work with each one individually. Now that's power in your hands!

The Outstanding & Completed Filters are available for all budgets regardless of whether or not they are linked. By default, we show all income and expense entries. You can also choose to view only the outstanding entries (those with an actual amount not yet entered) as well as both outstanding and completed entries.

Expense options are identical to income options with the exception of one additional option available to you that allows you to change the default category to use when adding new entries. We showed you earlier a quicker way to do this by simply clicking on the category description, but if you forget, the option is here as well. Keep in mind if you change an expense option, the corresponding income option is changed automatically to match your selection.

There are corresponding commands you can use for each of these options as well. They are listed in parentheses after the option description. Use the commands to save you from having to show the options panel, make your selection, and then return to the normal display. Commands are your friend and will make life easy for you.

WORKING WITH BANK CONNECTIONS

My Connections is an optional paid feature that will allow you to connect to you bank and pull in transactions. Contains many features beyond the scope of this book that take budgeting to the next level. Check our website for more details and available resources.

SPECIAL SETTINGS FOR EDUCATIONAL ACCOUNTS

Sometimes, it is easier and more fun to learn budgeting concepts in a classroom setting, where different ideas and approaches can be openly discussed and debated. We built special controls for educational accounts to make it as easy as possible to setup and teach budgeting concepts in a classroom setting. Educational accounts have the following additional features:

1. Ability to assign students to a classroom and period. This can be done one student at a time, or using the bulk import feature.
2. Ability to stage budgets so students in the class all begin exercises with the same sample budget material.
3. Ability to review student budgets to confirm they are grasping the material being taught.
4. Ability to clear out the class and start over as needed.

WHATS NEXT?

I could never finish this book and the *Budget Ninjas* system if I waited for every grand feature to be added. I will always be working to improve the system and to keep it relevant for the times in which we live. One of the great features about being online is that I can provide you these updates without you having to do anything (other than enjoy the new features).

We are always open to fresh new ideas and suggestions to make our products and materials better. Send us a note and tell us what you think of it or what you would like to see! We hope to be your partner for a very long time. Now it's time to go make some dreams come true.

THINKING OUTSIDE THE BOX

Back in the first week, I challenged you to think outside the box with a puzzle. Since then, you have had to think outside of the box several times while preparing your budget, and hopefully, you now have a budget you are working with and you are well own your way to becoming free of the financial pressures of life. Now, about that puzzle: all you have to do is draw your first line from the bottom-left dot straight up through the dots on the left side, continuing your line "outside" of the box. Your second line would then be a diagonal line as shown. Next, your third line is drawn across the bottom, and your final fourth line is another diagonal line to hit the remaining dots. See, it can be done! Just like creating your first budget, it can be done! Congratulations and good luck!

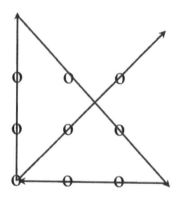

Our goal is to make budgeting as fun as possible. On our website, we will occasionally post a cartoon strip about our favorite family, the Smiths. The Budget Buddies comic series will surely bring a smile to your face. Check the news section of our website for recent posts, or like us or follow us on the social media outlets in which we participate. Here is a sample of the Budget Buddies comic series. Enjoy!

ACKNOWLEDGEMENTS

Many have helped contribute to this book in one way or another. Thank you all for being there for me, letting me run ideas by you, and sharing your ideas as they relate to personal finances. You'll never know how much you inspired me as I worked on this book and developed the online system. I really couldn't have done it without all your help. Thank you – especially to the love of my life Vickey Byrd!

Thank you Chris Spooner for the original ninja artwork.
http://blog.spoongraphics.co.uk/

ADDITIONAL RESOURCES

Over the years, I have found a few websites that have become very useful in my never-ending quest to manage my money better. Here are some links to websites you may find helpful as well:

www.paycheckcity.com
This site has free paystub calculators so you can see how your pay is impacted if you decide to change your deductions on the W4 form. It also has a link to help you fill out the W4 form.

ABOUT THE AUTHOR

Dennis Byrd, author, and founder of the Budget Steward paltform, has also held a career in the computer technology field for over a quarter of a century. Dennis served on the Board of Directors for his church as their treasurer and is active in providing financial counsel for many groups and individuals.

Over the years, Dennis has developed accounting and payroll software for several companies and has used those skills, along with his financial counseling experiences, to perfect his unique approach to home budgeting - building the Budget Ninjas system. Dennis has taught his ironclad home budgeting process to many groups, individuals, businesses, and non-profit organizations. Dennis Byrd has been happily married for more than 34 years to his lovely wife, Vickey. Dennis and Vickey live in Taylors, SC, and have two grown children, Katie and Daniel.

Made in USA - Kendallville, IN
1133929_9781523826407
07.08.2020 0801